MW00644033

STAY FOCUSED
Living Right,
Thinking Right

D. Clay Perkins, Ph.D.

Ancient of Days Publishing

February 28, 2017

ISBN 978-0-9987551-2-0 printed book
ISBN 978-0-9987551-0-6 ebook

DEDICATION

This book is dedicated to Dr. Darel Pruett, D. O.,
and his wife, Mary Pruett.

I am grateful for their love of Christ, family, and friends. I am honored to be among their many friends. The gift of a place to stay on Parker Drive in Islamorada, Florida, to write, rest, and fish, provided the right place at the right time to complete this writing project. You will never know how deeply appreciative I am for your generosity and love for others in your walk with Christ. May God continue to bless and use you, especially in your work with medical missions in HASTEN International.

What others are saying about
Stay Focused: Living Right, Thinking Right

Stay Focused provides commentary on and clarity to selected scripture. The author employs examples from his life to make the scripture real and relatable. As we read and ponder God's Word, we should be moved to make a difference in the lives of others for the Kingdom of God. Allow God's Spirit to work in your life through *Stay Focused*. God will use you to impact others for the Kingdom in more ways than you can imagine, yes, even "immeasurably more." I have been blessed by the writings of, and by knowing Clay Perkins. - Benjamin H. Allen

This book is magnificently written with an enormous amount of valuable information on survival and life skills and offers expert advice on how we should live our lives while here on earth. I believe that if individuals would follow the advice of the writer: What a wonderful world this would be. It also points out the importance of keeping God first and staying focused on how we treat others that do not look and worship like us. - Dr. Hezekiah Brown

This book will teach you how to handle painful moments in life. Clay speaks boldly and unapologetic about subjects affecting our community such as diversity and racism. This book will help guide you and challenge you to a better way of thinking and living. As a lead Pastor, this a great tool for sermonic illustrations. - Darrell Hairston, M.DIV

It has long been observed that "... of the writing of books there is no end." While this is certainly a factual observation, it does not claim that the need for books to be written will ever end. The need for books like this one by Dr. Clay Perkins will certainly always exist. Every generation needs to be exposed to devotional reflections on the truths of God's Word especially if those reflections are grounded in real life situations. Dr. Perkins weaves human interest stories from everyday life with nuggets of Biblical truth that illuminate the impact on our lives of taking God's Word seriously as our guide. - Ronnie J. Woolard, Professor of Bible, Mid-Atlantic Christian University

The words of this artistic and thoughtful publication speak to the heart and soul of the human spirit. It provides to the reader a "Spiritual GPS" to finding joy, peace, and the freedom to navigate the challenging conditions of life and still have joy. Well done! - Bishop Ernest R. Sutton

I have had the pleasure of working with Dr. Perkins for the past decade. This book represents an expression of his character and beliefs as a man of God. It will help you, "to be set for the defense of the gospel." Well done Clay. - Gene M. Langley

Clay Perkins is a multi-talented man. In these short devotionals, he pulls from his many spheres of experiences to give us fresh insights in The Word. How great to have them collected into one volume rather than having to wait until the next week to read them in the newspaper—now you can find the one that best fits your life for today—or read a number of them for a lift to start your day. You will not be disappointed. - William A. Griffin, former President, Mid-Atlantic Christian University

This book is a must read for anyone who sees their Christian faith as more than something just practiced for one hour in a church on Sunday mornings and who is frustrated and concerned about our world today. Interpreting biblical verses through powerful stories and personal reflections the author avers for the need for all Christians to become active members, in fact leaders, in the secular world. But this book is more than just a 'call to action'; it is also a 'how to book'. Citing the importance of Christian values for providing a way for all of us to move forward together, guidance is given in such areas as the value of diversity, voting, relations with our boss, stewardship, leading by asking powerful questions, accountability, serving the poor and the standards by which we should live our lives. Finally the author leaves us with a question and a challenge: Will we ever learn to love one another? - Joe W. Peel, Mayor of Elizabeth City, NC

Stay Focused is well written and focuses on today's issues dealing with real life situations. It is an awesome read. - Dr. Peter L. Kunkle

The best books do more than entertain us. Yes, they sometimes make us laugh, and that is a good thing. They also encourage us, because we all need encouragement, comfort us when we need comforting and challenge us to be better than we would otherwise be. In this book, Clay Perkins uses uncommon common sense and consistent reference to the timeless truths of Holy Scripture to do all of this. We will all be better for having read it. - Roger A. Brady, General (ret) USAF

These simple stories hold extraordinary meanings. In them you will find yourself and God. Read, relax and find an inner peace. - Robert L. Perkins, Jr.

In the ever spinning world we live in, it's hard to keep our focus on only one thing for long. In his book, Dr. Clay Perkins invites you to a table filled with a smorgasbord of delicious dishes that will satisfy your appetite for God. As you dine, you may laugh and you may weep. But it's okay, because the One who made you and sustains your life has invited you to His table. *Stay Focused: Living Right, Thinking Right* will leave your heart full and satisfied, and ready to invite others to the table. Bon appétit! - Gregory D. Hand

CONTENTS

ACKNOWLEDGEMENTS

I give deep appreciation to Melissa Lewis and Sandra Perkins. Their editing skills are extraordinary. Their ability to challenge every word I wrote with grace and convictions has and continues to improve my writing skills. This work would not be possible without them.

Special thanks to Eggroll Studios Creative Director, Dave Milam, for the book cover design. Thank you to Sandra Perkins for the cover photo. Thank you to coryfurlough.com for the author photo used on the back cover.

I am grateful to Trustees at Mid-Atlantic Christian University for a three month Sabbatical from the day to day operation of the University that it has been my honor to serve for over eleven years. With your help, this book has become a reality.

A special appreciation to one amazing woman who has been by my side for decades. You are truly a "wife of noble character" (Proverbs 31:10-31). Much love to you, Sandra Louise Sechrest Perkins.

PREFACE

This book is a collection of columns that were written for The Daily Advance, a newspaper in Elizabeth City, NC, from 2014 through 2016. These were not written to a Christian audience, but for the general reading public in the "Harbor of Hospitality." Like most small towns in America, Elizabeth City is mostly Christian, but very much a pluralistic society. The city is a great place to live with people from all walks of faith and even those with no faith perspective. If you have never visited the "Harbor of Hospitality," please come and see us, you will be glad you did.

It has been very fulfilling personally to have members of the community come up to my wife, Sandra, or to me, to express appreciation for the weekly column. It is an honor to play any role in encouraging others in right thinking or right living, helping others to stay focused. Now that the writings will serve a larger audience, it is doubtful that we will meet at a local restaurant or at a community event, but I will still love to hear from you.

I am thankful to Mike Goodman, Publisher and Executive Editor of The Daily Advance, who gave me this opportunity to write a weekly column. This religious column was limited to 400-600 words each week. I have served as the primary author, but from time to time have had guest writers, per the publisher's request. This book only contains my writings. The topics were inspirational by nature, but much a response to understanding what is going on in the world, particularly with insight into cross-cultural issues.

Each chapter (column) stands alone. I do not think that anything I have said or written is truly original. The reality of the truth found in Ecclesiastes 1:9 is real to me as to any author or speaker and great care has been given to appropriately cite references. But often, especially with anecdotally stories, original sources are simply unknown. Care was taken to identify true stories. Specific stories are from my life or the lives of those close to me that I love. (True Story) Some stories are clearly fictional and have been handed down through various speakers and preachers. (Anecdotal Story) In fact, is it my hope that many speakers and preachers will find a great story or two from this book to become one of their new "go to" stories used to inspire others. Scriptures are quoted from the New International Version of the Holy Bible.

At times, a story, or thought, is repeated in various chapters/columns. There are some columns that were clearly a reaction to current events. Many columns fell on holidays, and were written from that perspective. Many columns were from my speaking and preaching during those years.

At times, the writings are very introspective as I was working out my faith in a pluralistic society. The reader should remember these contextual factors. But each chapter/column remains very beneficial. The purpose of this writing is to serve others and to help us stay focused.

Serving Those Who Serve,
D. Clay Perkins, Ph.D.

CHAPTER 1. DIVERSITY AND DELICIOUS STEW

The body is a unit, though it is made up of many parts; and though all its parts are many, they form one body. So it is with Christ. 1 Corinthians 12:12 (NIV)

"Variety is the spice of life," we have often heard. In contrast, another axiom may feel more comfortable for many of us: "Birds of a feather flock together." Just look at the chaos we know as a banana split. There may be comfort in that same old vanilla cone, but there is often more joy in diversity like a banana split.

Higher education once taught us that the world was flat. Now we know better. Higher education, in the field of Sociology, has taught us that America should be a great melting pot. With all due respect, that thought is also wrong. Humanity shines best when one celebrates the diversity found around the corner and around the globe. A society good for all citizens is better represented by a stew pot, and not a melting pot.

When Momma made beef stew, those carrots were much better after being mixed with that meat ... those potatoes were great when they mixed with those onions ... that meat was far better after stewing with those vegetables. Nevertheless, those carrots never became meat. And those potatoes never became onions. But because of the diversity in the pot ... yum, it sure was great.

Those with deep spiritual heritage will remember the song, "Red and yellow, black and white, they are precious in His sight.

Jesus loves the little children of the world." We would do well to remind ourselves that in the end, we will be celebrating with people from "every tribe and language and people and nation" (Revelation 5:9b). Why not start the celebrating now with people from all walks of life?

I do admit I like people like me. After all, I like me. But I have learned the joy of relationships with people not like me. Love shines best when we respect others. Life is more complete when we honor others, their cultures, and ways of life.

Look at the simple, yet complex, example of our body: such a variety of parts with so many different functions. Alone, the parts cannot function; but when placed together, they can build a bridge, write a song, find a cure, and soothe the hopeless. The hand will never be a foot. And the eye will never be an ear. But where would the hand be without the foot? And where would the ear be without the eye? (See 1 Corinthians 12:12-31.)

Join me in enjoying the diversity found in our churches, our families, our friends, and our nation. Stay who you are. But let variety spice up your life and enrich it. You will be glad you did.

CHAPTER 2: THE YELLOW ROSE OF GRIEF

My comfort in my suffering is this: Your promise preserves my life. Psalm 119:50 (NIV)

You will increase my honor and comfort me once more. Psalm 71:21 (NIV)

She was very close to her mother. Her family was large, with seven siblings, yet she had a special relationship with her mother. Then her mother died unexpectedly.

Grief is never a quick process. This is especially true when the grieving is over someone you love so much. It is without end, until that special day. For Christians, grief is unique – it is pain confused by faith. Faith calls us to know what we hope for and to be certain of what we do not see. (See Hebrews 11:1.) Often we need to see the nail prints. We need to see that which cannot be seen.

She thought her prayer was one without faith, a prayer of a doubter. She prayed, "Lord, I want a rose!" Yellow roses were her mother's favorite. So she asked God, "If Mom is okay, and I know she is, send me a yellow rose from my mother on the one-year anniversary of her death to let me know for sure."

Her faith told her not to ask such a thing from God, not to tempt God, not to question God's timing. Her faith told her this sign was not needed. Her faith told her that she already knew, but somehow her heart would not listen. So her prayer was a request from her heart, a silent request between her and her God.

The day came. Had she allowed her emotions to override all common sense? Had she set herself up for more pain? Why did she do this? Why did she doubt? Her faith was strong, but her grief was also strong.

The day was anxious. Morning came with many good events, but no yellow rose. Afternoon came, and the lack of a gift from God caused the prayers to change. "God, I am sorry. I know that your Word is true. I know my mother is fine. My head, my faith will just have to convince my heart. God, thank you."

Then there was a call from her boss. "Meet me." She thought to herself, this day had been full, and this interruption would slow her down in closing out the day's responsibilities. Sensing her frustration, the reply came back, "I have something you want." The sight took her breath away. The God of the universe had honored her doubt. There before her was a single yellow rose. The giver was unaware of her silent prayer. To the giver, the rose was a thank you gift for a job well done. To her, it was a gift from God in response to the prayers of her heart.

God is the giver of all good things. He gives comfort in the time of grief. And sometimes, a yellow rose.

(True Story)

CHAPTER 3: PRAYER: HOW TO

I have not stopped giving thanks for you, remembering you in my prayers. Ephesians 1:16 (NIV)

For this reason I kneel before the father. Ephesians 3:14 (NIV)

... That you may be filled to the measure of all the fullness of God. Ephesians 3:19b (NIV)

What do you pray for? If you are like most of us, your prayer list consists of those who are sick, those who need a job, those who are in some current struggle, etc. These are good things to pray for, but are they the best things to pray for? Now, do not misunderstand – if I am sick, please pray for me. If I need a job, I need your prayers. However, such needs are but temporary.

I am increasingly convinced that the church today does not know how to pray properly. Prayer is not our getting something out of God. Prayer is God's getting something out of us. He desires our love, our trust, our total dependence on Him. We need only to look at the prayers in the Bible and model our own prayers after them.

This is a very dangerous concept. If you really begin to model your prayers after those found in the pages of God's word, your life, and the life of your church, might change forever.

For example, look at the prayer found in Ephesians 1:15-23. The prayer spoken was "so that you may know Him better" (Ephesians 1:17b). I wonder, what would happen if when we pray for someone to feel better or to get a better job, we also pray for that person to know God better. As Socrates is attributed with saying, "The unexamined life is the life not worth living." How true! But even more important, the unexamined faith is a faith not worth having. It is the obligation of man to know God better. It is the obligation of man to seek to God.

The prayer in Ephesians 3:14-21 was for us to know the fullness of God, to know just how much God loves us! Do you remember singing, "Deep and wide, deep and wide, there's a fountain flowing deep ad wide?" Just imagine, what if you prayed for your family, friends, neighbors, and co-workers to know how much they are loved by God, to "grasp how wide and long and high and deep is the love of Christ" (v. 18).

Now most, if not all of us, pray. The question is, do we pray for things that are temporary or for things that are eternal? Are we wise with our prayers? Knowledge is knowing that a tomato is a fruit, not a vegetable; wisdom is knowing a tomato does not belong in a fruit salad.

Let's know not only how to pray; let's be wise in what we pray for. Let's pray for the eternal as well as the temporary. Remember, prayer is not our getting something out of God. Prayer is God's getting something out of us – a totally dependent child.

CHAPTER 4: SATISFACTION OF MORE

Now to him who is able to do immeasurably more than all we ask or imagine, according to his power that is at work in us.
Ephesians 3:20 (NIV)

MORE. We live in a "more" society. We all want more. We really like more of this or more of that. If we have a boat, we want a bigger boat. If we have a job, we want a better paying job. If an investment is earning a single digit return, we want a double digit return. If our business is growing, we want it to grow more. If we have a good cell phone, we want the one that is coming out next month.

Our spiritual leaders often remind us that "more envy" is evil. They appropriately suggest that we should learn to be satisfied with our lives. Like Paul, we should learn "to be content whatever the circumstances" (Philippians 4:11). But alongside that contentment, we also realize that we are in partnership with "him who is able to do immeasurably more than all we ask or imagine" (Ephesians 3:20).

I like the way Agur states his desires before the Lord: "Two things I ask of you, Lord; do not refuse me before I die: keep falsehood and lies far from me; give me neither poverty nor riches, but give me only my daily bread. Otherwise, I may have too much and disown you and say, 'Who is the Lord?' or I may become poor and steal, and so dishonor the name of my God" (Proverbs 30:7-9).

So, perhaps, when we hear the words "immeasurably more" we need to "reboot" our minds to think not of things that are temporary, but of things that are eternal. God is ready to use ordinary people to accomplish great things so that others can know just "how wide and long and high and deep is the love of Christ" (Ephesians 3:18). God is seeking to have his love known to everyone through our lives.

So let's desire more. No, let's desire immeasurably more! After all we have the power of the Spirit of God at work in us. So I boldly say, "I want more." Let me be clear. I want so much more that you will not be able to measure it. I want more. Will you join me? Together let's look for more ways to make the love of God known. Let's take more time to help someone. Let's take more time to pray for someone. More time to love ... desiring more does not always have to be a bad state.

CHAPTER 5: THE POWER OF QUESTIONS

"Why are you searching for me?" he asked. "Didn't you know I had to be in my Father's house?" (Jesus) Luke 2:49 (NIV)

He said to them, "Why are you troubled, and why do doubts rise in your minds?" (Jesus) Luke 24:38 (NIV)

It has always amazed me that Jesus asked a lot questions. He often answered questions with a question. Why did he not just give a straight and simple answer? Would that have been better? A clear answer, and not a question, would have given better clarity.

The scriptures quoted above are two instances when Jesus answered a question with a question from the Gospel of Luke. In the first example, Jesus was answering his parents, who were likely quite annoyed with him since he had just caused them to be very anxious. Rather than answering their appropriate question, Jesus asked them a couple of questions. The second example occurred when Jesus' disciples were likely speechless. They were confused, startled, scared, and were thinking, "Is this a ghost?" They were not quite sure what to think or what to ask. So, what did Jesus do? He asked them a couple of questions.

Even when Jesus was asked the age-old question "What must I do to inherit eternal life," He seems to dodge the question. Jesus responded to the wealthy man's question by asking him a question, "Why do you call me good?" (Story in

Luke 18:18-30). Come on, Jesus, just answer the question. Please.

It has taken me decades to understand this simple reality modeled by the Master Teacher. Maybe it will not take you as long to accept this pedagogical axiom: Questions are often better than statements. Why? Questions will cause people to think. Statements cause people to agree or disagree.

I hate to admit it, but maybe I liked statements better than questions for years because I thought I knew something. I thought I had something to say. Maybe I just liked to hear myself talk. Or maybe I thought I was helping others to learn about God with my statements. In contrast, Jesus helped people learn about His father not only with statements, but also with lots of questions.

The truth is our God wants us to think. God calls us to come and reason together (See Isaiah 1:18), to ponder, to consider life, death, and life after death. He calls us to contemplate war and peace. God welcomes questions on pain and pleasure.

So, if you want to be a more effective teacher of the Bible, shouldn't you ask more questions? Do you want to help your employees to do their very best? Do you want your children and grandchildren to grow up to be good and to make wise choices? Why not follow the Master Teacher and ask more questions?

CHAPTER 6: SPIRITUAL WAR

Finally, be strong in the Lord and in his mighty power. Put on the full armor of God, so that you can take your stand against the devil's schemes. For our struggle is not against flesh and blood, but against the rulers, against the authorities, against the powers of this dark world and against the spiritual forces of evil in the heavenly realms. Therefore put on the full armor of God ... that I may declare it fearlessly, as I should. Ephesians 5:10-13a, 20b (NIV)

If you are seeking to live a spiritual life, do not be naïve: we are at war. We are in a spiritual battle. As we win battles, we can boldly tell others about the love of God.

Three stories from my life remind me we are in a spiritual battle.

The first story is a memory of going to a funeral years ago. The deceased was the spouse of a woman in the church I served. I had never met the man; he never came to church with his wife. He never cared for his wife or his children. When I walked up to view the man's body, I suddenly felt the presence of evil. It was cold. It gave me the chills. It was evil.

The second story is a memory from my trip to Haiti. Our hosts from the region told us very sternly: "Do not go out at night No matter what, do not leave the second floor of the building you are in until morning." Each night we heard the Voodoo drums. We heard the chants.

The third story is a memory from my trip to France, where I stood in some of the great cathedrals. In particular, I remember the amazement I felt touring Notre-Dame Cathedral in Paris. The architecture of Notre-Dame de Paris is stunning with its flying buttresses, statues (particularly of the virgin and child), and the gargoyles. The relics include things like the Crown of Thorns and Holy Nails. I stood in awe viewing the stained glass windows, the bells, and the pipe organ with over 7,000 pipes.

I was there that day with hundreds of tourists when I noticed over in the corner a very small group of believers worshiping God. They were worshiping the Creator, not the things created. The Spirit of God overwhelmed me, and I cried. A building that, through the ages, has guided people to know God had on that day more sightseers than worshipers.

My friends – this is war. And our battle is not of this world. Our fight is not with flesh and blood, but between evil and good. We fight so that good might prevail.

CHAPTER 7: SECRET GUILT

Blessed is the one whose transgressions are forgiven, whose sins are covered. . . . When I kept silent, my bones wasted away . . . Then I acknowledged my sin to you and did not cover up my iniquity. I said, "I will confess my transgression to the Lord." And you forgave the guilt of my sin. Psalm 32:1, 3a, 5 (NIV)

She was caught by her older sister. She was smoking a cigarette behind the shed. In her mind she knew she would pay for this. Mom had told her children not to smoke. But to her amazement, her older sister said nothing, absolutely nothing, to Mom. Wow, was her sister really going to keep her secret?

As the days passed and Mom was assigning chores, the older sister started using a phrase, "No, Mom, my sister will do that for me." Then she would look at her younger sister and whisper, "Won't you, Smoky?" For days on end, her older sister manipulated her. Any time she did not want to do a chore, she would tell Mom her sister would do it for her. Then she would quietly taunt the younger sister with, "Won't you, Smoky?"

She did not know what to do. Her "secret sin" was safe, but the price was high. The guilt. The mistreatment. The frustration of doing her chores and her sister's chores was driving her crazy. So, in tears, one day she told her mother the truth of her disobedience.

She will never forget what her mother said. "My child, I figured this out long ago. I knew you were smoking. I knew your sister knew you were smoking. What I did not know was how long you would allow your sister to torment you."

We do the same thing with our sins. We hide them. We allow Satan to torment us. To tell us we are not good enough. The evil one likes to remind us with the smoky smell of our mistakes. But please read all of Psalm 32. God knows we have sin. He is waiting to forgive us. He is waiting for us to stop listening to the Devil's lie when he whispers in our ear, "Smoky, you cannot be forgiven."

Rejoice and have an upright heart. Enjoy the forgiveness that comes from the Lord. He is willing to protect you. God will deliver you from torment and guilt and give you peace. (See also 1 John 1:9.) It is good to be forgiven by the Lord God Almighty.

(True Story)

CHAPTER 8: CHOSEN FIRST STRING

For he chose us in him before the creation of the world to be holy and blameless in his sight. In love he predestined us for adoption to sonship through Jesus Christ, in accordance with his pleasure and will – to the praise of his glorious grace which he has freely given us in the One he loves. Ephesians 1:4-6 (NIV)

God chose you.

Think about that Biblical truth. You and I have been chosen by God. The decision to do this was made long ago. It was planned. This intentional sovereign act was to allow us to be pleasing to God. He wants us to be holy and blameless in His eyes.

You and I are truly blessed. We are first string. We are number one.

Personally, I have no clue how that really feels in the world of sports. I come from a family of eight children. I have four brothers. When the high school coach heard there was another Perkins on the way, he was happy. Some of my brothers were very good at sports. But I remember the coach asking me after seeing me play: "Are you sure you are a Perkins?" You see, I scored a total of two points in my high school basketball career. On the playground when teams were chosen, I often I found myself in that dreaded position of being the last one picked. You can understand why I find myself very excited about being chosen by God.

God's love caused Him to choose us, to predestine our adoption process. While we may not be able to fully understand "divine election" even with unlimited words, we can understand that we have been chosen by God. God has been working forever on making us a part of His family. This adoption process started before creation. He adopted us through Jesus Christ because He wanted to; it brought Him great joy. It is His pleasure to serve us. So think about that for the rest of your life – God intentionally, at very high cost, has made it possible for you and me to be His sons and daughters. We are now in the family of God. His children.

Your childhood memories may be similar to mine, or you might have been a sports super star. It really does not matter. What does matter is that you have been chosen by God. You can know what it is like to be first string with God, to be His number one pick.

You are blessed.

CHAPTER 9: TIED UP

*Have confidence in your leaders and submit to their authority,
because they keep watch over you as those who must give an
account. Do this so that their work will be a joy, not a burden,
for that would be of no benefit to you.* Hebrews 13:17 (NIV)

He walked into the meeting with gifts. His managers
smiled. He gave them each a very nice pocket knife, they
thought in appreciation for a job well done, and it was. But the
unexpected gift had a double meaning.

The rest of the meeting was typical. The meeting was filled
with the inevitable tyranny of the urgent. There were reminders
of protocols and coaching on how to serve the customers.

At the end of the meeting, one manager spoke up and said,
"Thanks for the gift. These pocket knives are very nice." Heads
nodded in the room, and others took the opportunity to express
their thanks for the unexpected gift. "Why? What did we do to
deserve this?" some asked.

The boss spoke up and said, "I do appreciate all your hard
work. But you frustrate me a lot. The pocket knife should help
you with that."

"How?" they asked.

He replied, "The next time I call you and tell you to call me
and you say 'I am all tied up,' cut yourself free and call me." The
boss turned and walked out of the room.

We all have bosses. What are you doing to make their life a
joy? How are you responding to their requests? Are you second-
guessing every decision they make? Are you respectful? Do you

think you can do a better job? Would you like those who report to you to treat you the way you treat your boss?

God will hold us all accountable. So, whether your boss is a saint or a jerk, try to work hard to make his or her role as a leader a joy. Make it your goal to be the best employee ever and not the "Employee from Hell." Let's give our managers all the respect that is due to them and the office they hold. After all, it is not savvy to do anything else.

(True Story)

CHAPTER 10: WHO IS WATCHING?

But I tell you that everyone will have to give account on the day of judgment for every empty word they have spoken. For by your words you will be acquitted, and by your words you will be condemned. Matthew 12:36-37 (NIV)

I love boating and fishing. All boaters and fishermen know a common fact about these hobbies - you are always having to fix something. Sure enough, I found myself spending several hours searching websites looking for a replacement part for something broken that has not been manufactured for a couple of years. Found it. Now, to ruminate on whether it is worth fixing or whether I should simply replace it with a new item. The decision to spend money is not easy for me, so I put my decision on hold. And when I did, IT happened.

For the next week or so, every time I opened up anything on the web, ads popped up for "parts suppliers" to solve my every need. Even when I read the local newspaper online, numerous advertisers seemed to know that I needed their service to resume my boating and fishing addiction. I must admit, this cyber marketing stalking was, well, creepy.

Now, we all know IT is called "marketing." Mathematicians call it algorithm. I call IT creepy. It was as if I were being stalked to buy this one unique item. So be very careful what you do on the web. Many are watching and keeping records of everything you type.

God is keeping a record too. Therefore, we should be very careful what we say. Or think. Words matter. Thoughts matter. Everyone will give an account for every word. This thought may or may not be as creepy as internet marketing, but it should have your attention.

God's memory is better than any algorithm. The Bible is very clear: we are held accountable for our words. Paul builds on the words of Jesus and advises us to "take captive every thought to make it obedient to Christ" (2 Corinthians 10:5b). So before we must bite our tongues to prevent us from saying something we will regret, we should challenge our thoughts so that our tongues never get the opportunity to misspeak.

May all our words and thoughts be pleasing to God (See Psalms 19:14).

So, what have you been saying lately? What have you been thinking? Is it pleasing? What would the marketers try to sell you? Even more importantly, would God smile?

CHAPTER 11: THE DISCIPLINE WOODPILE

Endure hardship as discipline; God is treating you as his children. For what children are not disciplined by their father? ... No discipline seems pleasant at the time, but painful. Later on, however, it produces a harvest of righteousness and peace for those who have been trained by it. Hebrews 12:7 & 11 (NIV)

Discipline is rarely appreciated in the moment, but it can be treasured in the future. Discipline is timeless.

Dad was frustrated with his son's mouth. He was tired of the son's whining about all the hard work he had to do. Dad decided that this Saturday was workday and he would show his son what hard work really was like in hopes that his son would learn the reality of life.

Dad woke his son up very early, and they cleaned and fixed everything in sight. Anything and everything that possibly could be done was done. His son was a strong young buck, so he had no trouble keeping up with Dad.

Toward the end of the day, Dad was running out of things to clean or fix, so he told his son to move the woodpile from here to there. Muttering under his breath, the son began what was obviously busy work. Dad went inside for a break and dozed off. He woke up to his son standing in front of him, hands on his hips, saying, "I hope you're happy now, your wood has been moved."

Without saying a word, Dad got up, walked out to the deck, and surveyed the work his son had just completed. "Nope, I think I liked it where it was. Move the wood back to where you found it." Then Dad walked away. The son moved the woodpile again. When he was done, Dad asked him if he knew why he had to move the woodpile a second time. "Yea, because of my attitude and lip," was the son's curt reply. Very few words were exchanged between father and son for several weeks.

As a parent we often wonder if what we do to teach and discipline our children really matters. Are they listening? Do they understand? Will this tension ever end? Will our sons and daughters be normal one day?

Years later his son had his own teenagers and lived in another state. Dad had long forgotten about the woodpile, when over the phone his son told him, "Dad, I have no idea what I am going to do with my son. His attitude and lip are driving me crazy. Dad, I wish I had a woodpile!"

Lesson learned. As a society, are we still disciplining our children? Do we expect children and teens to obey? What stories will our children tell us about the discipline we gave them? If we skip a generation of discipline, what will result? Scripture is clear: discipline matters (see Hebrews 12:7-11). If we do not teach our children to obey us, whom they can see, how will they ever obey God, whom they cannot see?

I am thankful for the lessons I have learned from my father. I am eternally thankful for the lessons I have learned from my heavenly Father. If we learn from God's discipline, we gain righteousness and peace. Not a bad trade-off for short-term hardship and pain.

(True Story)

CHAPTER 12: VOTE

... if my people, who are called by my name, will humble themselves and pray and seek my face and turn from their wicked ways, then I will hear from heaven, and I will forgive their sin and will heal their land. 2 Chronicles 7:14

Blessed is the nation whose God is the Lord, the people he chose for his inheritance. Psalm 33:12

    Let me be straightforward. Christians should vote. Christians should promote political leaders that support biblical values. Be informed. Vote.

    Since the time of Christ, some spiritual leaders have encouraged their followers to void themselves of all political matters and focus on the eternal. These spiritual leaders have distain for any involvement in elections. After all, "Government, even in its best state, is but a necessary evil; in its worst state, an intolerable one," according to Thomas Paine.[1]

    On the other end of the spectrum, some spiritual leaders have politics at the core of their ministry. In my lifetime, the Rev. Martin Luther King, Jr., is a prime example of this passion. One example from antiquity would be the Prophet Amos. Dr. King often quoted Amos' words, "Let justice roll like a river, righteousness like a never-failing stream!" (Amos 5:24).[2]

---

[1] http://www.ushistory.org/paine/commonsense/sense2.htm

[2] http://www.drmartinlutherkingjr.com/letjusticerolldown.htm

For whatever reason today, some do not want their spiritual leaders coaching them on social political matters. At the same time, they want to hear from those who entertain them from Hollywood or from the world of sports. Why would we seek to silence spiritual leaders on such important matters but welcome commentary from others?

I have always enjoyed the definition of "politics" our former Secretary of State, Dr. Robert Reich, delivered with a smile at a conference I attended: "It is from the Latin word 'poly' – meaning 'many' – and 'ticks' meaning – blood suckers." No wonder we hear joking phrases like "Vote early, vote often." This admonition reflects the fact that many have lost faith in the political process. Our Republic is often inconsistent. Is the Republic governed by the rule of law, or are we governed by the rule of man? Do we have freedom of religion or freedom from religion? Does the glove fit? Does it matter what the definition of "is" is?

Has history repeated itself? Do we "call evil good and good evil"? (Isaiah 5:20). Are we living in a time when there is widespread social injustice, when the poor cannot stand, when the righteous are sold for silver, when we deny justice to the oppressed? And if we are living in such times, do we not need to hear from our spiritual leaders? Do we not need to hear a clear call to "Hate evil, love good; and maintain justice in the courts" (Amos 5:15) from our spiritual leaders?

It is very clear that the Bible encourages us to pray for our leaders in 1 Timothy 2:1-4. It is very clear that, at times, God is not pleased with those we have chosen to lead (Hosea 8:4). It is very clear that Jesus was passionate about social justice and righteous leaders.

But be very, very careful. God is not a supporter of donkeys, elephants, or bags of tea. Christianity is not a political party. The Almighty is passionate about justice, honesty, fairness, and leaders who will administer such so that we can live peaceful and quiet lives.

We should vote. We should speak out. We should respect others, even if they disagree with our thoughts or directions for a good society. Our governmental leaders whom we elect, or whom we allow to stay in office, can do great good – or great harm – for both individual and social justice.

So step into that voting booth. Pray. Think. Be informed. And then vote.

CHAPTER 13: A GOOD NAME

A good name is more desirable than great riches; to be esteemed is better than silver or gold. Proverbs 22:1 (NIV)

"All you have is your name. So don't lie boy." I can still hear my Dad say those words although he has been home (deceased) many years.

I went to college straight after high school. As my family's first generation college student, one of my first tasks was to find a job. I would not be a student athlete. I would be a student worker. After asking around, I decided to apply at a local grocery store. The wages were good, the hours were flexible, and I was told they liked students from the college I chose to attend. The college I attended was an elite faith-based college.

At the grocery store I met the manger and asked for an application. I had no more stated my name and where I attended college when he interrupted me, asking, "When can you start?" Those were indeed simpler times. Later, as I got to know the manager better, he told me that he hired me on the spot because of the good name of all the students he had hired from that local Christian university prior to hiring me. He found the students to be hard workers, honest, and faithful, but added with a smile, "At least, the majority of them were great workers."

I was benefiting from the reputation of the students who had gone before me. I had the advantage of following good people who had left a great impression in a very busy metropolitan grocery store. On weekends it was common to have very long lines at the cash register all day long. It was very hard, demanding work. Nevertheless, I worked very hard to be one of the best workers he ever had at that grocery store. Years later, when I left that job, he shook my hand and told me, "The reputation – the good name – of the students [of the college I attended] continues." I was happy to do my part.

So do you bring honor to your name? Do you bring honor to your organization? Your family? After all, a good name is all you have. Therefore, always do your best. Show up early. Stay late. Work hard. Make a name for yourself and those who will come after you to serve. Cherish, protect, and uphold your good name.

A good name is worth more than gold.

héros

CHAPTER 14: BUT GRACE

BUT because of his great love for us, GOD, who is rich in mercy, made us alive with Christ even when we were dead in transgressions – it is by grace you have been saved. Ephesians 2:4-5 (NIV)

BUT is a wonderful word in the English language. It tells the reader that there is a contrast with what has been said and what will be said. In the case of Ephesians 2:4-5, the contrast is huge, because the "but" – the difference – is caused by God's great love for us. I love the word "but," and especially as it is used in Ephesians, "BUT ... GOD."

Each of us was dead. We were dead because of sin in our lives. Spiritual death is separation from God (Isaiah 59:1-2). Being spiritually dead is the absence of God. The truth is: we were all dead because of sin (Romans 3:23).

God – because He loves us so much and is so rich in mercy – made us alive, even when we were dead. We serve a God who can give life to death. He raised a 12-year-old girl (Luke 8:49), a young man (Luke 7:11), and an old man (John 11) from the dead. He can do the impossible. In fact, He specializes in the impossible.

The contrast we all need to notice is this: even though we were dead, we are now alive. We were dead, 'BUT ... GOD' made us alive. Salvation is from the Lord (Jonah 2:9). And this salvation has a name: Grace. I love the old hymn, "Amazing grace, how sweet the sound that saved a wretch like me, I once was lost, but now am found, was blind, but now I see."

When the Bible speaks of justice, it is speaking of getting what one deserves. Oh my, we do not want justice from God. When the Bible speaks of mercy, it is speaking of not getting what one deserves. Oh, how sweet it is that God does not make us pay the price for our sins. When the Bible speaks of grace, it is speaking of getting what one can never deserve. Grace is free, a gift from God. Grace can never be earned. Grace is God blessing you with salvation simply because He loves you.

Yes, grace is amazing! Think about it. From God we do not get justice, even though we deserve it. Instead, we get mercy. But even better, we are given grace. In fact, in the future God plans to show off the incomparable riches of His grace by seating us with Him in the heavenly realms.

Grace may be hard to explain, but a word picture may help. Do you have a refrigerator? On it do you have artwork from a son or daughter, a grandson or granddaughter? In comparison, if God had a refrigerator, He would display you, your life, and your artwork. In his eyes, you are his greatest accomplishment. You are his artwork.

Be very thankful for the bold contrast of these two words: BUT ... GOD. Grace is amazing.

CHAPTER 15: THANKS TO GOD

Give thanks to the Lord, for he is good; his love endures forever.
1 Chronicles 16:34 (NIV)

Give thanks to the God of gods; his love endures forever. Give thanks to the Lord of lords; his love endures forever. ... Give thanks to the God of heaven; his love endures forever. Psalms 136:2, 3, & 26 (NIV)

I remain thankful for this nation (USA) and her Christian heritage. Reading the proclamations and prayers of our Presidents gives us the reason for the Thanksgiving season we celebrate.

"Whereas it is the duty of all Nations to acknowledge the providence of Almighty God, to obey his will, to be grateful for his benefits, and humbly to implore his protection and favor ... To promote the knowledge and practice of true religion and virtue, and the encrease of science among them and us--and generally to grant unto all Mankind such a degree of temporal prosperity as he alone knows to be best." President George Washington.[3]

"And I do also recommend that with these acts of humiliation, penitence, and prayer, fervent thanksgiving to the Author of All Good be united for the countless favors which He is still continuing to the people of the United States, and which

---

[3] http://lcweb2.loc.gov/ammem/GW/gw004.html

render their condition as a nation eminently happy when compared with the lot of others." President John Adams.[4]

"They are the gracious gifts of the Most High God, who, while dealing with us in anger for our sins, hath nevertheless remembered mercy. It has seemed to me fit and proper that they should be solemnly, reverently and gratefully acknowledged as with one heart and voice by the whole American people; I do, therefore, invite my fellow citizens in every part of the United States, and also those who are at sea and those who are sojourning in foreign lands, to set apart and observe the last Thursday of November next as a Day of Thanksgiving and Prayer to our beneficent Father, who dwelleth in the heavens." President Abraham Lincoln.[5]

"As we gather in our communities and in our homes, around the table or near the hearth, we give thanks to each other and to God for the many kindnesses and comforts that grace our lives. Let us pause to recount the simple gifts that sustain us, and resolve to pay them forward in the year to come." President Barack Obama.[6]

The proclamations of our Presidents remind us that the Sovereign One is the giver of all good things. May our leaders never forget that it is God that has so richly blessed this nation. May we always have leaders who first give all of the honor and credit to God. As citizens of this country we should pray for our leaders and for our nation. Together let us thank God for this great country we live in with all her freedoms and privileges.

May we, as individuals, also pause and give thanks. Consider writing a "proclamation and prayer" as you celebrate

---

4
http://www.pilgrimhallmuseum.org/pdf/TG_Presidential_Thanksgiving_Proclamations_1789_1815.pdf

[5] http://www.wallbuilders.com/libissuesarticles.asp?id=4082

[6] http://www.whitehouse.gov/the-press-office/2011/11/16/presidential-proclamation-thanksgiving-day-2011

Thanksgiving in America each year. Even though the document will likely never be available on-line inside some archive, it can make an impact on your family and friends. Start by writing a simple preamble – a few sentences about God's loving-kindness toward your family. Quote the scripture above if you are at a loss for words. Then at some point during the day start with the youngest to oldest and have everyone in his own hand writing simply state one or two things he is thankful for. Then at the bottom put the date and have everyone sign the document. Make copies for everyone. Perhaps several generations from now someone will read your family's proclamation and remember you and yours and how you took the time to thank God, who is so good.

God has blessed this nation. May we bless God with our prayers, comments, and proclamations of thanks giving.

CHAPTER 16: PEACE | HOME

BUT NOW in Christ Jesus you who once were far away have been brought near through the blood of Christ. Ephesians 2:13 (NIV)

When the weather turns cold each year we begin to think again about the homeless in our area and across the nation. As it gets colder, our hearts and minds automatically think about those who do not have the ability to stay warm because they have no home. Those who are homeless need us to intervene, to give them a hand up, and to provide them with a safety net.

Before Christ, each of us was homeless. We did not belong. We were excluded from the warmth of citizenship. We were foreigners needing someone to intervene so that we could find a home.

As an educator, I am always asking my students to compare and contrast, an exercise that requires students to think critically. A part of learning this skill of critical thinking is to study grammatical relationships among words. In this case – Ephesians 2:13 – there is a conjunction, "but," immediately followed by an adverb, "now." The word "but" tells the reader that there is contrast between what has been said and what is now being said.

You were once homeless – but now – you have a home. You were once unwelcomed – but now – you are welcome. You were once illegal aliens – but now – you are citizens. You once did not belong – but now – you belong.

Because we are now fellow citizens and members of the family, we live in peace. This change in our status is made possible by Christ. Christ himself is our peace (Ephesians 2:14). Christ made peace (Ephesians 2:15). Christ preached peace (Ephesians 2:17). You see, when we belong to the household of God, we have peace. As an old saying goes: "Peace is not the absence of pain, but the presence of God."

We are all fellow citizens now, God's holy temple, seeking to give the world peace. This belonging to the household of God is for all people, every tribe, every nation, and every language. Remember a song of your childhood, "Red and yellow, black and white, they are precious in his sight, Jesus loves the little children of the world"? You belong to one big, colorful family of God.

This is his purpose: to bring us together in him. God no longer lives in a tent. God no longer lives in a building. God no longer lives far away in the heavens. Now he also lives in his people. He lives in us – the church – God's holy temple – his family. And he wants us to offer homes to the homeless. Peace to those in pain. We are his.

We once had no home – but now – we are at home with God. We once had no peace – but now – we are at peace with God.

CHAPTER 17: CHRISTMAS | GIFTS

And then they opened their treasures and presented him with gifts of gold and of incense and of myrrh. Matthew 2:11b (NIV)

... faith, hope, and love. But the greatest of these is love. 1 Corinthians 13:13b (NIV)

Giving gifts is fun. I remember one year, when my two sons were young, we did the 12 Days of Christmas leading up to December 25. On the first day there was one gift. The second day, two gifts. The third day, three, and so forth. I think I was more excited than they were. On another Christmas we did gifts each Sunday of Advent. Then there were the years of special gifts – musical instruments, special Bibles, etc. I have wonderful memories of giving gifts to my sons.

Christians give gifts as a reflection of God's gift of His son. If you want to lessen some of the commercialism and consumerism most of us fall prey to at Christmas time, here are three timeless gifts you can give your children and those you care for every year.

Give the gift of faith. Your faith in Christ. Make sure you share with them your faith in Christ. "Faith is being sure of what we hope for and certain of what we do not see" (Hebrews 11:1). Share with your children and those around you the reason for the season. Have you ever thought about giving a gift to God? Malachi 2:15 gives us one gift God is looking for: He wants spiritual grandchildren. The good Lord above is asking us to share our faith with our children, our grandchildren, and all the children of the world so that He can have godly offspring.

Give the gift of hope. This inane world where prejudice is stubborn, peace is elusive, and pain is persistent is just not fair. This barbaric world of beheadings needs hope. We all need the confident assurance that God can give hope even on this crazy planet. "But those who hope in the Lord will renew their strength. They will soar on wings like eagles. They will run and not grow weary, they will walk and not be faint" (Isaiah 40:31). God's hope allows us to soar like a majestic eagle, to run marathons, and walk through this life's aches with self-reliance because we are not facing this world alone, our hope is in God. Giving your family hope that God will take care of you is a lifelong gift.

Give the gift of love. Love is a verb. Love is action. We find the practice of love in the "one another" passages in the Bible. Love is: one body, members of one another (Romans 12:5), devoted to one another (Romans 12:10), honor one another (Romans 12:10), same mind with one another (Romans 15:5), accept one another (Romans 15:7), instruct one another (Romans 15:7), greet one another (Romans 16:3-6, 16), serve one another (Galatians 5:13), carry one another's burdens (Galatians 6:2), bearing with one another (Ephesians 4:2), submit to one another (Ephesians 5:21), and encourage one another (1 Thessalonians 5:11). How genuine Christmas would be if we love one another in these ways.

While I am very glad I gave gifts to my sons when they were young, my guess is that they, like me, do not remember what they got for Christmas when they were 10 years old. I pray they remember and cherish these important timeless gifts that we sought to give them every Christmas and all year long. May the gift of faith give them the reason for the season. May the gift of hope allow them to face life, which is often full of challenges and pain. May the gift of love guide them in raising their children and in treating everyone with respect and kindness.

So this, and every, Christmas give the gifts of "faith, hope, and love. And the greatest of these is love" (I Corinthians 13:13).

CHAPTER 18: MONEY | STEWARDSHIP

The wicked borrow and do not repay, but the righteous give generously. Psalm 37:21 (NIV)

You have heard of "the bucket list." On my bucket list is "doing an infomercial." You know, those commercials we all hate and love at the same time. The ones that offer some amazing gadget or product that will transform our lives. These are products that "no one can live without." The price is only $99. "But wait," today only the price is not even $49; "but wait," this fantastic offer is only $19.99. "But wait," if you order today we will double your offer. I really want to do an infomercial. I even know what I want to pitch – wealth creation.

On my bucket list is pitching wealth creation. I have four easy, simple, basic steps that work over and over again. They are:

One: Spend less than you make. Do this for a long time, a really long time, like, years.

Two: Avoid debt. Seriously, if you cannot pay cash, do without. When you can afford to buy then pay cash.

Three: Save. And then save more. And then save even more.

Four: Give. Be absolutely ridiculous in giving. Be ridiculously joyful about helping others in this world.

And before you know it, you will create wealth.

I am the son of a truck driver, who was the son of a share cropper. There is no silver spoon in my mouth. I have often told people, "Yes, I have always had two challenges in life. Number one, I was not born with a silver spoon in my mouth. Number two, when I married I did not fix problem number one."

But everyone reading this column can create wealth. You cannot create wealth by tomorrow, but in the years to come, you can. Yes, I know you are more accustomed to ministers talking about the evils of money. The "eye of the camel" (Matthew 19:24), the "love of money" (I Timothy 6:10), and more, and, indeed all those warnings are true.

But in the same book we find the parable of the talents in which the rich man is the hero (Matthew 25) and another scripture in which the wise man leaves an inheritance for his children's children (Proverbs 13:22). And these passages are also true. Balancing and allowing the bible to interpret the bible is important.

John Wesley (1703-1791), founder of the Methodist church, within the Reformation Movement, is often quoted on stewardship. His simple message to "Gain all you can," "Save all you can," and "Give all you can" is as savvy today as the first time he preached it.[7] His simple biblical messages caused a redemption and economic lift of entire people groups.

The truth is that money is not "the" main thing, but money is "a" main thing. Wealth is amoral. By itself wealth is neither good nor bad. Money can do so much good, like providing food, shelter, and clothes for you and your family. Money can support churches, ministries, colleges and universities, and serving those in need. On the other hand, the love of money has caused many a good person to fail. Some have chosen to acquire it in unethical or illegal ways and spend it for evil purposes. But wealth itself is not the culprit.

I will likely never mark off my bucket list doing an infomercial, but I hope I can help many good people to create wealth. I have seen the good that money can do for family, faith, and society. I know the heart of many who have created

---

[7] http://www.umcmission.org/Find-Resources/John-Wesley-Sermons/Sermon-50-The-Use-of-Money

wealth, and still they are righteous. So, build wealth by spending less than you make, avoiding debt, saving, and giving. Then you can be an extraordinary instrument in God's hands for good.

CHAPTER 19: GRIEF

… weeping may stay for the night, but rejoicing comes in the morning. Psalm 30:5b (NIV)

See You at the House.

Years ago my life was interrupted by a miracle. It was the going home of a saint, my mother. She experienced the greatest miracle of all, going home. One of her common phrases was, "See you at the house." I can still hear my mother's voice saying this.

Miracles always come through the doorway of pain. The greatest miracle is the resurrection of our Lord Jesus Christ. It came through the doorway of the crucifixion. To go home to Jesus is the greatest miracle we experience. Mom left this home in the arms of the man she eloped with after almost 55 years. Dad was holding her and said he knew the moment when her spirit left for home. I am sure he did.

Her death was sudden and unexpected. In retrospect, she had been preparing her husband and her children for years. She knew her time to go home was near.

The miracle is I can still hear her voice saying, "See you at the house."

Miracles and pain go together. This reality is such a paradox. One thing about death and grief is it sucks. I know my mother would wash my mouth out with soap for using such a word. Good thing she's gone home. It is such an ugly word. But grief and death are so ugly. To touch and look at a body when the spirit has gone home is ugly. It is such a vulgar experience. Death and separation are vulgar. Satan's illusion of grandeur is vulgarity at its best.

I know she's home. But my pain is still real. How could one who ministers to those in need have been so blind to the depth of such pain? How could I have been clueless as to how much it hurts to experience a miracle? I had no concept of what people go through when they say good-bye for now to someone they love.

The miracle is I can still hear her voice saying, "See you at the house."

Miracles and priorities go together. What directions can come from pain? I listened to her grandchildren, as we gathered to grieve and say goodbye, as they read poems of respect and love for someone who taught them so much by simply living her life in Jesus before them. We watched her grandsons carry her coffin to lay a shell to rest. Dust to dust. Death has a way of refocusing priorities. What a miracle! Family, faith, love, and creating memories are now new and fresh priorities and commitments. Now health is important. Nothing matters but family, and living out your faith in your family. Now it is important to love your spouse, and to love your children. Is it not odd that death reminds us to live? Death reminds us what real life is all about.

The miracle is I can still hear her voice saying, "See you at the house."

Oh, the joy of being in Jesus while grieving my mother! Being a Christian in such a terrible time provides so much strength. How can one endure this miracle without Christ? To have no hope in a hopeless situation must be devastating.

Oh, the joy of knowing that she is home! To be absent from the body is to be with the Father. Precious are those who die in the Lord. She is home and waiting for her loved ones to join her. Mom is waiting in the arms of Jesus.

Oh, the joy of knowing that life goes on! What a privilege to dance the dance of life. To love. To be loved. To know Christ. To share Christ. To be a part of a big family.

Oh, the joy of going home! Perhaps the greatest miracle of all is to go home to Jesus. To enter into heaven singing praise to Almighty God. Going home is the ultimate miracle.

Oh, of the joy of the memory of her voice saying, "See you at the house." Oh, the joy of saying, "Mom, see you at the house."

CHAPTER 20: THINK BEFORE YOU SPEAK

My dear brothers and sisters, take note of this: Everyone should be quick to listen, slow to speak and slow to become angry.
James 1:19 (NIV)

Once again in my lifetime I see the images of riots in an American city. It is hard to imagine anger that is so strong that it leads to destruction, even to the destruction of oneself. It is disgusting, despicable, damnable, and disappointing. It sickens me to see the depth of evil that humanity can sink into.

What if society actually followed one brief passage from God's Word found in James 1:19? What if we took note and followed this important principle from James, the half-brother of Jesus? What if those leaders in the public arena, those leaders in our pulpits, and those leaders among us in our communities actually took note of these simple, yet powerful words? What if we actually did this?

"Everyone should be quick to listen." Take time to listen to people's stories. Listen long enough to know their pain and their joy. Listen long enough to know them. Everyone needs to be heard. Everyone is a child of God. God listens. God cares. So why shouldn't you?

"Everyone should be slow to speak." Words matter. So holding your tongue in the heat of the moment is savvy (Proverbs 10:19). The tongue can be very tough to tame (James 3) and there are times when it is best to put a muzzle on your mouth (Psalm 39:1-3). Be very careful with your words. Not only should we be slow to speak, but when we do eventually speak, we should speak the truth in love (Ephesians 4:15). We should say only that which is mutually beneficial (Ephesians 4:29). As Christians we should take any words we use and hold them captive to make them obedient to Christ (2 Corinthians 10:5). After all, a word or a ruling aptly spoken is like apples of gold on a platter of silver (Proverbs 25:11).

"Everyone should be slow to become angry." There is anger that leads to destruction. We have seen ugly accounts of destructive anger reported on the news. Conversely, there is anger from injustice that can lead to positive, peaceful, and productive change. We need more of this anger that is used to bring about good. Be very careful with your anger. Do not allow anger to control you. Make sure that you control your anger.

Consider being quick to listen, slow to speak, and slow to anger. Do we not realize that we have two ears and only one mouth? Do we think that what we are going to say is really that important? Do we think that what our fellow man has to say is really that unimportant?

Allow me to simply state the obvious given our national context. Social injustice and racism still plague us. I long for the day when "justice rolls on like a river, righteousness like a never-failing stream!" (Amos 5:24) Those who would make their living on race-baiting need to be unemployed and not in positions of authority. And those who earn their living seeking peace and justice need to be gainfully employed and in positions of influence. Police are to be respected and obeyed. When an officer of the law makes a mistake, and some will, they are to be held accountable. Peaceful protest is to be respected and honored. Thugs who riot and destroy property and persons are to be held accountable. To quote a historical leader who understands: "Darkness cannot drive out darkness; only light can do that. Hate cannot drive out hate; only love can do that." Martin Luther King, Jr.[8]

---

[8] Martin Luther King, Jr. *Strength to Love, 1963.*

Given that we are once again seeing images of riots, one would be savvy to remember the words of James as well as these words from the Prophet Micah: "He has shown you, O man what is good. And what does the Lord require of you? To act justly and to love mercy and walk humbly with your God." (Micah 6:8)

CHAPTER 21: CHEERFUL GIVERS

God loves a cheerful giver. 2 Corinthians 9:7b (NIV)

But store up for yourselves treasures in heaven, where moths and vermin do not destroy, and where thieves do not break in and steal. Matthew 6:20 (NIV)

We were young, dumb, and broke. Looking back, I am not sure if a bank would have given us a loan for this used car, but the owner was a friend, and he insisted that we did not need a bank, he would carry the note. About half way through the payments for the car we were told to stop making payments. We were confused. Our payments were on time, and we had not missed a single one. Thinking he wanted the car back, we protested. We had probably never met a cheerful giver at that stage in our lives. What he was trying to tell us was, "Keep the car. Stop making payments. We love to give to others. Have a great day." Wow. Someone was being very generous, and my wife and I were the recipients of a car for which we had paid only about half of the agreed-upon price.

That was one of the times in my life that I experienced a cheerful giver. Cheerful givers are amazing. They give out of their heart. They are not always people of means, but they are always people who mean to do well. They are intentional. They are disciplined. They love.

I learned a long time ago that people fall into two categories: Givers and Takers. Where do you fall? Are you a giver? Are you a taker? Is your first thought, "What can I do? How can I serve?" Or is your first thought, "What can I get? What will this do for me?" Be honest with yourself. Where do you fall? Are you a giver? Or are you a taker?

President Kennedy's words to us as citizens of the United States still ring true today, "Ask not what your country can do for you; ask what you can do for your country."[9] Or does this simple message still ring true today? Have we become a nation of citizens who want their government to give them one more thing? Do we look for one more handout? One more special tax break? One more exemption?

An old preacher story finds its setting in medieval Europe when a man walks up to a construction site. "What are you doing?" he asked the first man. "I'm cutting stone." He walks up to the second. "What are you doing?" "I am a stone mason." He walks up to the third worker and asks the same question, "What are you doing?" "I am building a cathedral!" All three men are working on the same job site, doing the same work, but each with an entirely different perspective. Those who choose to be givers in life build cathedrals. Others are tradesmen. Others, sadly just cut stones. Choose wisely.

Why not choose today to be giver? In so doing, the long-term benefits are plentiful in this life and the next.

(Anecdotal Story)

---

[9] John F. Kennedy inaugural speech, https://www.jfklibrary.org/JFK/Historic-Speeches.aspx

CHAPTER 22: AMERICA'S JULY 4

I urge, then, first of all, that requests, prayers, intercession and thanksgiving be made for everyone – for kings and all those in authority, that we may live peaceful and quiet lives in all godliness and holiness. 1 Timothy 2:1, 2 (NIV)

Life is best lived in peaceful and simple quiet moments. One of my favorite such moments is when I'm sitting on my screened back porch watching the sprinkler water the garden. The importance of quiet moments cannot be overstated.

I am struck by a quiet moment during our American Revolution when John Adams wrote a letter to his wife, Abigail, reflecting on his day, July 3, 1776, "I am apt to believe that it will be celebrated, by succeeding Generations, as the great anniversary Festival. It ought to be commemorated, as the Day of Deliverance, by solemn Acts of Devotion to God Almighty. It ought to be solemnized with Pomp and Parade, with Shews, Games, Sports, Guns, Bells, Bonfires, and Illuminations from one End of this Continent to the other from this Time forward forever more."[10]

Adams understood that what was about to take place called for both solemnity and celebration. I think Adams would smile today as fireworks explode from small towns to big cities, around lakes and oceans, in backyards and on street corners in

---

[10] Massachusetts Historical Society, Adams Family Papers, http://www.masshist.org/digitaladams/archive/doc?id=L17760703jasecond

honor and celebration of our independence. July 4th is our national holiday. Happy 4th of July!

So as you celebrate, please take time to enjoy life's simple pleasures and quiet moments. Spend time with family and friends. Enjoy all the food and festivities your heart desires. But also remember that we are truly blessed as a nation by our God. You can both party and pray. You can celebrate life and give thanks to God.

In the same letter to his wife, John Adams wrote, "You will think we transported with Enthusiasm but I am not. – I am well aware of the Toil and Blood and Treasure, that it will cost Us to maintain this Declaration, and support and defend these States."[11]

The price for our celebration today and tomorrow is very high. War is common. Peace is elusive. So pray for our leaders - from the White House to the local sheriff's office - on this day. These men and women in positions of authority are leaders ordained by God to govern our lives. They need our appreciation. Pray for our President. Pray for your Mayor. Pray for all our leaders. Pray that our leaders in authority will make wise decisions so that you and I can … "live peaceful and quiet lives in all godliness and holiness" … enjoying simple moments such as waving the red, white, and blue.

---

[11] Massachusetts Historical Society, Adams Family Papers, http://www.masshist.org/digitaladams/archive/doc?id=L17760703jasecond

CHAPTER 23: WORDS MATTER

For the ear tests words as the tongue tastes food. Job 34:3 (NIV)

Words matter. Words have meaning. Words are important. Words are vital to social harmony and a good society. Words give guidance on what to do and what not to do.

A story has been handed down that a young man was confused over the meaning of the words "complete" and "finished." What was the difference between the two words? Why more than one word, if they both have the same meaning? So he wrote Webster and asked for clarification. The reply came: "Young man, there is a significant difference in 'complete' and 'finished.' Allow me to explain. If a man marries the right woman, he is complete. If a man marries the wrong woman, he is finished. And if the right woman finds the man with the wrong woman, then that man is completely finished."

Words clarify. Words provide understanding. Words communicate. It is no wonder, then, the scripture tells us that a word aptly spoken is like an apple of gold on a platter of silver (Proverbs 25:11). The right word at the right time can bring great healing. The wrong word at any time can do great harm.

Years ago I listened to a very spiritually mature 80-year-old man, with tears in his eyes, tell me a story about words that were spoken to him when he was in his early twenties, words that were not aptly spoken. These words that were spoken were uttered by well-intended dragons. On the other hand, I have seen in the faces of individuals the healing and peace brought by the right words spoken at the right time.

When talking with children, we tell them a surface is hot – do not touch. We use the appropriate words to warn them: do not play in the road, eat this – do not eat that. We use words to clarify what will do them harm and what will be good for them. We do this because we love them.

We who are Christians are called to use words to communicate love, mercy, and grace. We should use words to communicate warnings of harm to humanity, as well, always speaking the truth in love (Ephesians 4:15) because we do not want to see others in pain. We want them to avoid suffering and hurt.

But do not be surprised if our friends do not like our warnings. Most of us do not like to be corrected or told no. And some do not want to be told that words really do matter, that they have meaning, and their meaning gives them importance – a function, a role to fulfill. Being salt and light to the world does not always make us popular. But when we love others, we tell them the truth even if we fear the truth will not be well received.

However, there are considerations given for sharing truth. Take, for example, the admonition found in Ephesians 4:29: "Do not let any unwholesome talk come out of your mouths, but only what is helpful for building others up according to their needs, that it may benefit those who listen." Think first. Ask yourself: Will my words bring encouragement? Will my words bring peace? Will my words build my relationship with this person? Will this person benefit from what I am about to say? And most importantly, will my words bring everyone closer to God?

As King David of old said, "May these words of my mouth and this meditation of my heart be pleasing in your sight, Lord, my Rock, and my Redeemer" (Psalm 19:14).

(Anecdotal Story)

CHAPTER 24: SHOW SOME RESPECT

Show proper respect to everyone. I Peter 2:17a (NIV)

Whatever happened to respect? I mean, true respect. True respect such as when one defers to the preference of others. True respect shown when one remains civil and friendly even if one cannot agree in any way with someone?

Have we become a people who demand that others think and act just like we do? Do we demand that others eat and drink the same things we do in the same ways? Have we lost the ability to respect diversity in culture? Do we now demand that everyone live out their faith in their business, family, and church in a way that pleases everyone? Have we lost common sense? Has "common sense" become the most uncommon thing there is?

Respect for others used to be common when satisfying our passions. If you are not of Jewish descent or practice, you would not go to a Kosher deli and demand pork. That would be unthinkable. That would be disrespectful. And if you do not share the Muslim faith, you would not go to a coffee shop with Muslim proprietors and expect to have bacon-wrapped pastries. I can respect those who do not share my passion for swine. I cannot understand it, but I do respect their rights. Why would I even consider suing them or demanding they go against their practice on how to live out their faith? How have I been harmed in any way? Do I not know that if I want baklava I would go to the appropriate vendor that sells baklava? And if I want bacon on my doughnut, I know a great place to go. Just ask me. How am I being mistreated by having to go to a different store?

Respect for others used to be common when living out our faith. Allow me to share two examples. Years ago when my bride and I were choosing how to live out our young Christian faith and become one in marriage, it would not have crossed our minds to demand that others outside of our faith perspective participate in our celebration. We knew Protestants were not allowed a Catholic wedding. No priest should be expected to endorse our matrimony.

I led a prayer service, in the Washington DC area, in which half of the audience was Muslim. The Muslims attending knew it was a Christian service. They listened, they participated, and they expressed deep appreciation after the service for being accepted and allowed to participate. This service happened during the Muslim celebration of Ramadan, a time in which they fast from sunrise to sunset. This Christian prayer service they attended was held on a Sunday afternoon and, even though they were living out their faith by fasting, they brought baklava, fruit, and drinks for the Christians attending to enjoy. Not one Muslim ate the refreshments that they provided, but they wanted to thank the Christians for allowing them to attend the Christian prayer service. We Christians enjoyed their respectful gesture, and the baklava was excellent.

Christians have deeply held beliefs that affect how we live our lives. These beliefs influence the way we run the businesses we own, or the way we behave on the job. They affect the way we dress, work, eat, behave, play, and relate to others. We live in a society that often will not respect us, in a culture that will, at times, demand we change long-held and deeply felt beliefs. Members of that society may think that our beliefs mean we hate them, but nothing could be further from the truth. We love them.

So out of love, let us be careful not to return disrespect with anything but respect. Give others the gift that our God gives them: free will. And just maybe, by showing respect, we can be change agents, and the common-sense practice of respect will become common again in society.

CHAPTER 25: COEXIST

Peacemakers who sow in peace reap a harvest of righteousness.
James 3:18 (NIV)

One God and Father of all, who is over all and through all and in all. Ephesians 4:6 (NIV)

There is an interesting bumper sticker that has been around for a while: COEXIST. Perhaps you have seen it. It has the symbol of some of the major religions of the world: Islam, Buddhism, Science, Judaism, Paganism, Wicca, and Christianity. Often the tag line is: God is too big to fit into one place. Often this slogan is used to promote world peace. I find this idea intriguing. It is worthy of our consideration as a pluralistic society and as Christians.

Let's consider both sides of - "ifs."

If this use of "Coexist" means to respect all people regardless of their faith. If this slogan is to remind us to love those who are different whether by skin pigmentation, manner of dress or hair style, life style choices, ethos, and more, with acts of kindness and common courtesy. If this saying helps us to live in a pluralistic society in peace. If this prevents those with different lifestyles or faith perspectives from being tossed from tall buildings, beheaded, burned, blown up, maimed, murdered. If this is a simple and bold call for peace and not war. Is this is asking everyone to have respect for one another in all areas of life such as family, faith, business, pleasure. If this causes us to be remember that God created us with free will, giving man the right to choose him or to reject Him. If this gives us the freedom to practice our faith as we see fit in this country and other countries. Then by all means, we should COEXIST. This is very good. And I am for this, and you cannot change my mind.

On the other hand, if the use of "Coexist" is meant to express that all faiths are equal, then how can Christians accept this well intended slogan? If it is saying there is more than one way to God, then what do we do with the words of Jesus when he says, "No one comes to the Father except through me" (John14:6)? If this slogan is saying all gods are equal, what do we do with "You shall have no other gods before me" (Exodus 20:3)? If this is encouraging us to understand and accept that we can worship other deities, how can we, in light of so many teachings found in scripture (Exodus 20:4, Matthew 4:10, Luke 4:8, John 4:23)? If we do conclude that scripture is open to private interpretation, how do we reconcile our conclusion with 2 Peter 1:20, since God has a clear message for his people? If this slogan is saying that all faiths are right and all faiths are equal, how can that be, when the scripture says there is only one (Ephesians 4:4-6)? If the contingencies in this paragraph are what is meant, then, by all means, we should not COEXIST. This is very bad. And I am not for this, and you cannot change my mind.

CHAPTER 26: CITY ON A HILL

You are the light of the world. A town built on a hill cannot be hidden. Matthew 5:14 (NIV)

Once again the American presidential election cycle has begun. Politicians from all sides will articulate in great platitudes how they will fix America. They will invoke word pictures from a plethora of sources to convince us, the voters, that they alone are the answer to all the woes in America and around the world. Many will even quote the Bible.

A word picture often cited by politicians is that America is to be "the city on a hill" from Jesus' words in a sermon known as the Sermon on the Mount (Matthew 5-7). Politicians talk of America being a role model for all nations. America is to be an example of virtue, freedom, peace! America is God's country! America is exceptional! It is a nation worthy of being lifted high.

It appears the use of the phrase "city on a hill" in American politics started with an English Puritan lawyer named John Winthrop. Winthrop served as Governor of what is now known as New England overseeing a wave of immigration into the newly found colony. In a sermon he delivered in route to the Massachusetts Bay Colony, he was encouraging the colonists to live righteously, to be a model of Christian charity, and to be that "city on a hill" as they built a new government:

For we must consider that we shall be as a city upon a hill. The eyes of all people are upon us. So that if we shall deal falsely with our God in this work we have undertaken, and so cause Him to withdraw His present help from us, we shall be made a story and a by-word though the world. [12]

Our 35th President, John F. Kennedy, used the phrase just prior to becoming President in a speech to the Massachusetts State legislature calling for government to be noted by courage, judgment, integrity, and dedication:

Today the eyes of all people are truly upon us – and our governments, in every branch, at every level, national, state and local, must be as a city upon a hill – constructed and inhabited by men aware of their great trust and their great responsibilities. [13]

The 40th President, Ronald Reagan, used the same phrase in his farewell speech to inspire Americans to be exceptional. "I've spoken of the shining city all my political life, but I don't know if I ever quite communicated what I saw when I said it. But in my mind it was a tall proud city built on rocks stronger than oceans, wind-swept, God-blessed, and teeming with people of all kinds living in harmony and peace, a city with free ports that hummed with commerce and creativity, and if there had to be city walls, the walls had doors and the doors were open to anyone with the will and the heart to get here. That's how I saw it and see it still."[14]

I deeply appreciate that our leaders will borrow a phrase from the Bible, especially from Jesus' Sermon on the Mount, to inspire us. And, I, for one, who have travelled to over 16

---

[12] The Winthrop Society, Praeservare ET Transmittere, http://winthropsociety.com/doc_charity.php

[13] John F. Kennedy Presidential Library and Museum http://www.jfklibrary.org/JFK/Historic-Speeches.aspx

[14] The Reagan Library https://reaganlibrary.archives.gov/archives/speeches/1989/011189i.htm

D. Clay Perkins

different countries, do find America to be exceptional. However, as a minister and educational leader, I do cringe a little wondering if we are missing Jesus' original point.

Are not Christians to be the city on the hill? Are not Christians to be the salt and light for the world? Are not Christians to be the hands and feet for the love of God? Are not Christians to do good for others so that others will notice and give credit to God? Why do we assign to this great country that which Jesus assigns to his people? Should not the church be the example of charity that will lead every tribe, nation, and language to know God? Why are we giving to our nation a responsibility – a calling – that belongs to the church?

Therefore, as you listen to your favorite candidate for President and find that he or she quotes the Bible, listen carefully and know the difference between the role of good citizens at work in this great country and the role of the God's people at work in the world.

CHAPTER 27: SERVING THE POOR

When you are harvesting your field and you overlook a sheaf, do not go back to get it. Leave it for the foreigner, the fatherless and the widow, so that the Lord your God may bless you in all the work of your hands. Deuteronomy 24:19 (NIV)

For even when we were with you, we gave you this rule: "The one who is unwilling to work shall not eat." 2 Thessalonians 3:10 (NIV)

Serving the poor is complex. I will not pretend that I have all the answers. But I will not neglect to speak about one of the answers. How we love and minister to the poor is paramount to our living out our faith before God and our fellow man. How we minister to the poor will always be a challenge. The poor will always be with us (Matthew 26:11, Mark 14:7). But should not the expectation of "work" be a part of the solution, especially in America?

Serving the poor is personal for me. I am the son of a truck driver, who was the son of a share cropper. I know poverty. But having seen, as an adult, with my own eyes and having smelled with my own nose the slums in other countries, I must be honest and report that I do not know poverty.

The struggle of serving the poor in America is nothing new. In the Jamestown colony we have records of John Smith's struggle to manage life among the colonists. Smith referred to the Apostle Paul's exhortations from Second Thessalonians quoted above, which can be summarized: No work. No eat. He did provide a caveat for those who were sick or disabled or otherwise indisposed. That is a safety net for those who cannot work. His logic was that honest, hardworking men should not carry those who are able but simply refuse to work.

Since the founding of our country, from the New Deal to the War on Poverty, we have strived to help the helpless as a society. Indeed, this is both a noble and an appropriate fight. But is not one possible solution found in the four letter word "work?"

What do you notice about the advice given to farmers in early Jewish history? Were they not to leave the crops that they missed and the crops from the edge of their fields for those less fortunate? Did you notice that the farmers were not to harvest the crops, process them, and then give them to the poor? Are not the foreigners, fatherless, and widows to work harvesting the crops left on the ground? Does doing this work give dignity?

I am grateful for the many individuals and groups that serve those who need help. Many farms, both large and small, have a food program built on this Jewish tradition. I am grateful to live in a nation that tries to provide safety nets for those in need. I do ask, "What did you do this week to serve the less fortunate?"

Serving the poor is a complex issue. It is a task the church should always perform as a role model to society at large. There are many other examples from scripture to guide us in this ministry. But is not work to be part of the solution?

CHAPTER 28: THE CODE

The decrees of the Lord are firm, and all of them are righteous. They are more precious than gold; than much pure gold; they are sweeter than honey, than honey from the honeycomb.
Psalm 19:9b-10 (NIV)

What is the code? What is the formula for a good society? What are the standards that we all should live by? Is there a right way to live together as people from different tribes? What is the secret to living together in peace? How are we to act as free people? Do we have the code right in front of us? Has the code been revealed long ago in righteous decrees from the Lord?

Israel, as a nation, had long been held in slavery according to the Bible and History. The twelve tribes of Israel were experienced in living under tyranny. They were accustomed to Egypt being their master. But now, for the first time in centuries, they were free. So how do they now live, without a slave master telling them what to do?

God had taken his people out of slavery. They are now free. Free to do as they wish. Free to make decisions. Free at last! But freedom brings chaos. So God provides a code for living as a free nation. A guide for people who are free to make their own laws. Free to determine their own destiny. This is the foundation for The Code. The Ten Words. The Ten Commandments. (Exodus 20:1-17). These are overarching principles for all people to live in peace, as free men and free women. Many suggest these guidelines are as relevant today as ever before. Many suggest these guidelines are irrelevant, that man has evolved beyond these archaic principles.

When our nation was formed, many of the founders based the forming of our laws for our freedom on this very same code given to the nation of Israel. Listen to our first president, George Washington: "Reason and experience both forbid us to expect that national morality can prevail in exclusion of religious principles."[15]

And our second president, John Adams, "Our Constitution was made only for a moral and religious people. It is wholly inadequate to the government of any other."[16]

And again from our fourth president and Father of the Constitution, James Madison: "We have staked the whole future of American civilization, not upon the power of the government, far from it. We have staked the future of all our political institution upon the capacity of mankind for self-government; upon the capacity of each of us to govern ourselves, to control ourselves, to sustain ourselves according to the Ten Commandments of God."[17]

Now there are those who strongly believe we should move beyond these standards. They are passionate that the Ten Commandments are not relevant. But if they are not relevant, an obvious questions arise: What will the new standard be? Who will decide the foundational laws for people from various backgrounds to live in peace and freedom? What is the code for a good society?

As Christians we should know our code. But not only should we know the code, we should also have the same

---

[15] https://berkleycenter.georgetown.edu/quotes/george-washington-on-the-importance-of-religion-to-political-prosperity-in-his-farewell-speech

[16] https://founders.archives.gov/documents/Adams/99-02-02-3102

[17] http://blowthetrumpet.org/JamesMadison.htm

passion for keeping the Ten Commandments as those who wish to void the commandments.

And God spoke all these words: "I am the Lord your God, who brought you out of Egypt, out of the land of slavery. "You shall have no other gods before me. "You shall not make for yourself an image ... "You shall not misuse the name of the Lord your God ... "Remember the Sabbath day by keeping it holy. ... "Honor your father and your mother ... "You shall not murder ..."You shall not commit adultery ..."You shall not steal ... "You shall not give false testimony ... "You shall not covet. Exodus 20:1-17 (NIV)

CHAPTER 29: JESUS GIVES THANKS

I will give thanks to the Lord because of his righteousness; I will sing the praises of the name of the Lord Most High. Psalm 7:17

Could there be a better holiday than Thanksgiving? The smell of food alone is enough to make any person smile. I enjoy family and friends eating together and thanking God for all the blessings he has given.

Many families have the tradition of asking everyone around the table to share one thing he or she is thankful for before the big meal begins. Everyone smiles when the children mention everything from their moms and dads to their pets or favorite toys. Everyone smiles and cries when someone mentions a loved one that is no longer at the table. Typically, everyone has something to say thanks for, even the grump of the family.

Thanksgiving is a rich tradition in America. It became a federal holiday in 1863 with President Abraham Lincoln's setting aside the last Thursday in November as a national day of thanks, "a day of Thanksgiving and Praise to our beneficent Father."[18]

While American Thanksgiving is not a Biblical tradition, it is in harmony with our nation's Judeo Christian ethos and heritage. And being a Jesus follower, I can't help but ask, "What was Jesus thankful for?"

---

[18] https://www.abrahamlincolnonline.org/lincoln/speeches/thanks.htm

Jesus thanked God for meals. "And when he had given thanks" (Matthew 15:36b). In this context Jesus is feeding the four thousand after performing many miracles of healing on the mountainside. He was moved with compassion for the crowds of people. Jesus was concerned that they had not eaten for three days. He did not want to send them away hungry. His disciples' search for food secured only seven loaves of bread and a few small fish. From that small amount of food, all ate their fill and still there were seven basketfuls of leftovers. In the midst of many miracles that day, we find that Jesus still expressed thanks for the simple basic need of every human: food.

Jesus thanked God for hearing Him. "I thank you that you have heard me" (John 11:41b). In this context Jesus is raising Lazarus from the dead. He had returned to a hostile area to make known God's power so that people would believe. Some thought Jesus was confusing death with sleep, but Jesus was not confused. He had a plan and purpose for the people in this time of grief. As Jesus prayed, the dead man came back to life and walked out of the grave. His plan was for them to believe. At the beginning of his prayer, he thanked God for hearing His prayers.

Jesus thanked God for providing salvation. "After taking the cup, he gave thanks" (Luke 11:17a) and "he took bread, gave thanks" (Luke 22:19a). In this context Jesus is participating in the Passover, a rich Jewish tradition of remembering God's rescuing the nation of Israel from slavery. Now Jesus will be a sacrificial Lamb of God. He will be salvation for all people from every tribe and every nation. He thanked God – even though He knew the pain and shame He would endure – that He would be salvation. He would be Savior.

So this Thanksgiving, consider sharing these three things that Jesus was thankful for: food, answered prayers, and salvation. Remind those at your dinner table that if you asked Jesus "What are you thankful for?" His response would be clear. His response would range from the simple to the miraculous. He thanked God for everyday needs and our eternal need. So thank God for everything: your food, whether it is simple or extravagant; His answers to your prayers in times of joy and grief; and the eternal salvation of all mankind through Jesus Christ our Lord.

CHAPTER 30: PEACE | CHRISTMAS

Glory to God in the highest heaven, and on earth peace to those on whom his favor rests. Luke 2:14 (NIV)

Seldom does a man read the obituaries . . . and find his own name listed as deceased. He was one of the few. His brother, Ludvig, had died, and reporters seeking to be first with the story had made a mistake. So Alfred Bernhard Nobel had the rare privilege of reading his own obituary, and what he read caused a paradigm shift in his life. Alfred was a successful businessman in his own right as a Swedish chemist and engineer. He is credited with the invention of dynamite and modern plywood. It was his armament manufacturing that caused the reporter to write: "The merchant of death is dead"[19] and "Dr. Alfred Nobel, who became rich by finding more ways to kill more people faster than ever before, died yesterday."[20]

But Albert Nobel took note. He spent the rest of his life seeking to change his legacy. He began what is now known as the Nobel Peace Prize. He left the vast majority of his estate to launch into perpetuity his cause – peace.

Peace remains elusive. Evil continues to rear its head in various names. For generations persecuted groups have included those who follow God, both Jews and Christians. War

---

[19] http://www.britannica.com/biography/Alfred-Bernhard-Nobel

[20] Golden, Frederic (16 October 2000). "The Worst And The Brightest." *Time.*

remains constant as mankind fights over ideology, land, warped religions, and more. America's fighting "Radical Islam," "ISIS," or whatever name you call this evil, is not new; it dates back at least to the First Barbary War of 1801. Terrorist tactics have remained a plague throughout human history. Mankind continues to look for more ways to kill more people faster. Genocide, barbaric behavior, and beheadings are not new to our generation. This will not be the first Christmas when evil looms.

At Christmas, peace is a common theme. We find this word on greeting cards, holiday displays, songs, and more. While most of us will never receive the Nobel Prize for peace, we can do our part for peace in our neighborhood and around the world.

Think about it. What can you do to leave a legacy of peace? How can you give peace a chance to thrive? Can you do the simple things, like opening doors, saying please and thank you, treating others with respect regardless of nationality or faith? Can you say Merry Christmas to those who believe in Christ? Can you say Happy Hanukkah to those of Jewish faith? Can you do the noble things like pray for peace, pray for your enemies (yes, even those who would seek to harm you and your way of life), pray for our governmental leaders (those who have authority over you), and seek to live in peace with all people – even those who do not share your belief?

If so, then maybe that old earthly song will be true, "Let there be peace on earth, and let it begin with me." If so, then maybe the song the angels sang at Jesus' birth will be true, "Peace on earth." May God's favor rest on all the people of the earth.

Shalom.

CHAPTER 31: WHAT CHRISTMAS IS ABOUT

Today in the town of David a Savior has been born to you: he is the Messiah, the Lord. Luke 2:11 (NIV)

"Save the bows!" I can still hear those words from my childhood. There is typically one in every family, someone seeking to manage money or to be environmentally friendly by re-using bows on Christmas gifts. I must admit; I, too, developed this savvy habit.

Today I wonder if we need a rally cry to save the original meaning of Christmas. Charlie Brown asked that question in 1965, in a TV special, "A Charlie Brown Christmas: "Isn't there anyone who knows what Christmas is about?"

Have we made the simple complex? Have we made the giving and receiving of gifts the main thing? Is the desire to have the biggest and best production in our houses of worship distracting from the message? Are we passing on to the next generation the tyranny of the pursuit? How can we return to the simple celebration of the Christ Child?

Consider how you can return to sanity this Christmas. This will be different for each family. You will have to determine how to keep the Christmas story alive in your own family. Why not do some extra acts of kindness? Volunteer in a local non-profit seeking to serve other people, with no personal benefit other than the joy of serving. Look for those who have no extended family and invite them into yours. There is always room for one more. Can you simplify or reduce gift giving (unless you plan to give me a new fishing rod and reel)? Maybe just focus gift giving on the children. Can you, or a child, read the Christmas story from God's Word when your family and friends gather? If everyone has "stage fright," then use an audio Bible. Why not ask that family member who is a musician to play a song when your gather? Not everything needs to be a Hollywood production. Consider having a birthday cake and sing "Happy Birthday" to baby Jesus. By now you have probably thought of several more things you can do.

Here are some of the things we did when we had children in the home, changing activities through the years: With extended family we always read the Christmas story and prayed for our family. We used Advent candles, reading scriptures and praying, then giving the children presents each week. We read "The Twelve Days of Christmas," giving gifts for the twelve days leading up to Christmas. We attended Christmas productions in both small and large churches. We always displayed a nativity. There was more. Each family should be intentional in keeping the real story alive.

So, yes, save the bows. That is savvy. But even more important, be very, very sure to save the true meaning of Christmas.

As Linus told Charlie Brown,

And there were shepherds living out in the fields nearby, keeping watch over their flocks at night. An angel of the Lord appeared to them, and the glory of the Lord shone around them, and they were terrified. But the angel said to them, "Do not be afraid. I bring you good new that will cause great joy for all the people. Today in the town of David a Savior has been born to you: he is the Messiah, the Lord. This will be a sign to you: You will find a baby wrapped in cloths and lying in a manger." Suddenly a great company of the heavenly host appeared with the angel, praising God and saying, "Glory to God in the highest heaven, and on earth peace to those on whom his favor rests." (Luke 2:8-14, NIV)

CHAPTER 32: DOING GOOD

*Do not be deceived: God cannot be mocked. A man reaps what
he sows. ... Let us not become weary in doing good, for at the
proper time we will reap a harvest if we do not give up.
Therefore, as we have opportunity, let us do good to all people,
especially to those who belong to the family of believers.*
Galatians 6:7, 9-10 (NIV)

Ugh. Not again. Another Christmas party where instead of
enjoying the holidays, he ended up practicing medicine. He
really did not mind, but the person went on and on and on. He
ended up taking out his tablet and journaling the symptoms of
the person and then sending in a couple of prescriptions to a
pharmacy. He advised his patient to come into the office within
the next 30 days for follow up if the problem persisted. After
the conversation was finally over and the person left his side, he
looked at his phone and noticed he had spent about 30 minutes
with this person. He turned to his good friend, a lawyer, who
had heard the entire conversation, waiting patiently and asked,
"I have a good mind to just bill them for a medical consult. What
do you think? Can I do that?" His friend, a lawyer, said one
word, "Yes." After that, they simply enjoyed the party.

The following week when he was back in his office, he
thought, why not. After all, his lawyer said he could and people
need to be held accountable for taking advantage of his good
nature. So, he instructed his staff to bill for the impromptu
medical consultation at the Christmas party.

Doing good for others is often not convenient. And, as the story suggests, the one receiving the act of kindness needs to also consider the inconvenience placed upon the giver of kindness. But for now, let's not focus on the recipient, but rather on our doing acts of kindness. After all, the scripture cited above is really not very hard to understand. You and I should look for opportunities to do good. Opportunities to do acts of kindness for others with no expectation of reward are in front of us every day.

Recently I have seen random acts of kindness that people might not even remember if you asked them to rehearse some kindness they had done. A lady dropped a dollar or two and did not notice, and several people behind her in line spontaneously said, "Ma'am, you dropped some money." A grandson brought donuts to the hospital's ICU staff that had been treating his grandmother for days just to say, "Job well done. Thanks." A yard is cared for as a family is in another state where a loved one is being treated for critical health issues. The people in the drive-through lane are surprised to learn that the folk in the car ahead of them paid for their fast food breakfast. It makes me smile when I see people doing good while expecting nothing in return.

These opportunities are around us every day. What acts of kindness have you done this week? Why not do good whenever you can? Why not be a giver and not a taker? Can you think of ways you can serve others? Serving others while expecting nothing in return can be fun, even when it is not convenient.

Back to the story of the doctor with the impromptu medical consultation at the Christmas party who decided to bill the patient. A week or so later, the doctor found in his mail a bill from the lawyer for the impromptu legal advice rendered. The scripture cited above really is not very hard to understand. You and I will reap what we sow.

(Anecdotal Story)

CHAPTER 33: RELIGIOUS FREEDOM

Let justice roll like a river and righteousness like a never failing stream. Amos 5:24 (NIV)

Religious Freedom Day and Dr. Martin Luther King Day often fall very close to each other on the calendar. When this happens, I think that Dr. King would smile. Dr. King's call for justice was guided by his faith, his theological education, and the liberty to act on those convictions.

We are a nation that has always cherished religious freedom. On January 16, 1786, the Virginia General Assembly adopted Thomas Jefferson's Virginia Statute for Religious Freedom. This statute became the foundation for our first amendment of the Constitution of the United States of America.

"Congress shall make no law respecting an establishment of religion, or prohibiting the free exercise thereof; or abridging the freedom of speech, or of the press, or the right of the people peaceably to assemble, and to petition the Government for a redress of grievances."[21]

Upon this bedrock of religious freedom, Dr. King acted. We have freedom of religion, but our nation is not free from religion. We are free to exercise our religion in the church, marketplace, and government. So Dr. King did just that.

---

[21] http://www.usconstitution.net/xconst_Am1.html

Did you know that during the Birmingham civil rights campaign, Dr. King required every participant to sign a pledge committing to do ten things?[22] We Christians have a history with the number "ten." Allow me to share a couple of the commitments required by Dr. King.

> Number 1: Meditate daily on the teachings and life of Jesus.
>
> Number 3: Walk and talk in a manner of love, for God is love.
>
> Number 4: Pray daily to be used by God in order that all men might be free.
>
> Number 8: Refrain from the violence of fist, tongue, or heart.

How much better would our nation be if the civil protests of today had leaders that would have their people commit to items like those Dr. King required, especially Number 8. Martin Luther King Day and Religious Freedom Day go hand in hand. May America always have leaders that will "Let justice flow like a river and righteousness like a never failing stream" (Amos 5:24).

---

[22] http://ncronline.org/blogs/road-peace/50-years-birmingham-pledge-nonviolence-still-inspires

CHAPTER 34: CREATOR

In the beginning God created the heavens and the earth.
Genesis 1:1 (NIV)

... So God created mankind in his own image, in the image of God he created them; male and female he created them.
Genesis 1:27 (NIV)

Then the Lord God formed a man from the dust of the ground and breathed into his nostrils the breath of life, and the man became a living being. Genesis 2:7 (NIV)

Eureka! We have finally done it! We now have constructed the process by which we can create mankind. The scientists were so proud of themselves. And then it hit them like a brick wall: We do not need God anymore! We have been able to clone animals for a while, but with this new breakthrough, we can now create humans. We are like God.

But, they wondered, who will go tell God? They selected their top two research scientists to inform God that he is no longer needed. Mankind could now create men and women from the dust of the ground, just like God.

The meeting started out well. God did not seem upset. He was not bothered by their newfound ability to create and simply gestured, "Show me." So the confident scientists reached down to gather the dust, only to be interrupted by God: "Excuse me, get your own dust."

The arrogance of mankind is nothing new. In the biblical record we seen this when we humans built a tower to try to reach God (Genesis 11:1-9) and when kings and rulers plotted for power (Psalms 2) over land and authority, only to have the Almighty laugh at their pretentiousness.

Biblical history is not the only example of man's self-importance. World wars have been fought over grabs for power and land. We have built cities below sea level and then wonder why they flood again and again. Nations have spent billions building manmade islands and then on rebuilding them. Man's arrogance is seen in attempts to save endangered species, which even comedians mock. Species have come and gone throughout earth's history. Hollywood has made millions on movies about parks with extinct animals from the Jurassic period. Do we really want dinosaurs in our woods? It is almost as if we have made saving animals, saving the planet, and fighting climate change and global warming a religion, all the while knowing that a good volcanic eruption and the normal effects of animals have as much or more effect on the climate as human ever had or will. And why are we so sure about the climate 100 years from now but not as certain about the weather 10 days from now? We continue to be a very arrogant lot.

Now be careful. It is certainly wise to do the best we can with the earth we have. But also be careful to remember this: mankind at our best is not qualified to be God, not even with a lower case "g."

(Anecdotal Story)

CHAPTER 35: HOME | HEAVEN

Consequently, you are no longer foreigners and strangers, but fellow citizens with God's people and also members of his household. Ephesians 2:19 (NIV)

Then I saw 'a new heaven and a new earth' ... And I heard a loud voice from the throne saying, "Look! God's dwelling place is now among the people, and he will dwell with them. They will be his people, and God himself will be with them and be their God. 'He will wipe every tear from their eyes. There will be no more death' or mourning or crying or pain, for the old order of things has passed away." Revelation 21:1a, 3-4 (NIV)

One of my favorite professors in higher education is Dr. Albert Einstein. There is perhaps no greater icon in academia. His disciplines were physics and philosophy. He is known for several theories, including general relativity and E=mc2. His many awards include the Nobel Prize in Physics and Time Magazine's "Person of the Century." He renewed his walk with God in the sunset of his life. A picture of Dr. Einstein with his crazy white hair hangs in my office.

A story is told of him traveling on a train. When the conductor came through taking tickets, Dr. Einstein fumbled around but could not find his ticket. The conductor assured him it was not a problem, that he was confident that a man of his stature had purchased a ticket. The conductor told him not to worry, just to sit back down and enjoy the trip. Dr. Einstein nodded in appreciation, and the conductor continued through the train car collecting tickets. Just before leaving the train car, the conductor looked back, and there was the distinguished Dr. Einstein on all fours obviously looking for his ticket. He rushed back and insisted, "Dr. Einstein, I know who you are, and I am confident you bought a ticket." Dr. Einstein stood up, brushed off his coat, and thanked the conductor again. Then he said, "Young man, I, too, know who I am. What I do not know is where I am going."

As we live our Christian lives in today's culture, we need to know not only who we are, but also where we are going. The old hymn is true, "This world is not my home, I'm just a-passin' through; my treasures are laid up somewhere beyond the blue. . . . if Heaven's not my home, then, Lord, what will I do?"

Christians are pilgrims in a foreign land. Thus, we should be very careful not to cherish the things of earth too dearly. Our sights are set on heaven. We are longing for home. And if we are, then our days of worry, pain, tears, and grief are more bearable. Our days of struggles and hardships are manageable. It is savvy to know who you are and where you are going.

(Anecdotal Story)

CHAPTER 36: GENTLEMEN

Submit to one another out of reverence for Christ. Ephesians 5:21 (NIV)

Have we lost the art of being a gentleman? Should men treat ladies with respect and dignity? Has our fast-paced, hypersensitive culture and our ever-changing social norms caused us to be foolish? I, for one, think we are very ill advised not to raise our young men to be gentlemen. Ladies are to be treated with high esteem.

I am not talking about limiting women in professions, pay grades, or rights. Women are free to choose their direction in life. Free to write their own story. Rather, ladies are to be admired no matter what path in life they have chosen. Ladies, you do yourself no favors when you shun chivalry, mistakenly equating it with a limitation, something holding you back. Chivalry, or having a gentleman submit to you out of respect, and your freedoms in Christ are not mutually exclusive.

Whether you are in a relationship or not, let us consider the fine art of being a gentleman. Let us bring back etiquette! While I could have consulted Hartley's book on etiquette, which was a complete guide for a "gentleman's conduct in all his relationships towards society containing rules for etiquette,"[23] I

---

[23] Cecil B. Hartley, *The Gentleman's Book of Etiquette and Manual of Politeness*, 1860, http://www.gutenberg.org/files/39293/39293-h/39293-h.htm

chose instead to ask the ladies in my workplace for tips on how a gentleman should treat a lady.

Opens doors. Warms and scrapes the car on snow days. Gives jacket when it's cold. Gives up his seat. Listens. Prays for her. Communicates without looking at his phone. Values opinions. Checks for danger. Offers to carry boxes, heavy items. Assists with putting coat on or off. Keeps confidences. Is dependable. Is honest. Kills spiders. Stands when a lady arrives or leaves. Uses good table manners. Walks beside her, not ahead of her. Speaks politely. Celebrates/acknowledges special occasions. Always lets her know if he will be more than 10 minutes late. Pays for meals and movies. Allows her to go first. Holds hands. Washes her car. Shows respect. Offers a hand to help when stepping down. Makes sure she gets inside before leaving. Fills vehicle with gas. Holds/shares umbrella. Compliments her.

This is a great list. Thanks to the ladies who supplied it.

Men, let's be gentlemen every day to every lady in our lives. And if you are fortunate enough to have a special lady in your life, may you treat her like a queen. And by so doing, are we not making our own lives, as well as the lives of those around us, better by submitting to one another? Is this not what Christ would have us to do?

CHAPTER 37: VEG-O-MATIC

My dear brothers and sisters, take note of this: Everyone should be quick to listen, slow to speak, and slow to become angry.
James 1:19 (NIV)

I cannot believe my mother did this to me. After all, I was her son. She, of all people, knew of my love for French fries. She knew that to me French fries were the primary food for life. My mother had the nerve to give our Veg-O-Matic food chopper to my younger sister. How dare her! This food cutter sliced thin and thick pieces, diced, julienned, and, best of all, made French fries. Would I ever be able to forgive her? As a teenager, I loved the Veg-O-Matic, made by K-Tel.

I learned an important lesson from that Veg-O-Matic. Once you cut the potato into French fries, you cannot put the potato back together. So you need to be very careful.

So, too, it is with our words. We need to be very careful what we say. Careful about when we speak. Careful about what we speak of. Words matter, and once they leave the mouth, they can never be taken back. No matter how sorry you are that you spoke them, no matter how much you wish you could take them back, you cannot.

That is why the scripture is clear on this topic. We are told to speak the truth in love (Ephesians 4:15). Yes, people deserve the truth, no matter how painful. But they should hear truth in the context of love. It is also clear that all words are to be mutually beneficial to others (Ephesians 4:2). I can still hear my mother say, "Boy, if you cannot say anything nice, bite your tongue." I cannot tell you how many times I wished my tongue would have bled rather than the words escape. Indeed, we are to be kind and compassionate with all things, especially our words (Ephesians 4:32). So, would those who are going to hear what you are about to say consider your words kind? Would they consider them compassionate?

No wonder another writer of scripture told us to be slow to speak and quick to listen. (James 1:19). Or, as one silly adaption of that truth says: You have two ears and one mouth, so perhaps you should listen twice as much as you speak.

I cannot believe my mother did this for me. You see, I was not shy in sharing my disappointment that my younger sister was given the Veg-O-Matic. My words were not mutually beneficial, even though I was just kidding with her and my sister. And to this day I do not know where Mom found one, since Veg-O-Matic by K-Tel had long since been out of production, but years later Mom surprised me at Christmas with a Veg-O-Matic of my own! I still use it decades later.

My love affair with French fries remains. Even more important, I hope my passion to remember remains – to remember that words matter, and, that once they leave my mouth, I cannot take them back.

CHAPTER 38: SERVING OTHERS

Not so with you. Instead, whoever wants to become great among you must be your servant, and whoever wants to be first must be a slave – just as the Son of Man did not come to be served, but to serve, and give his life as a ransom for many.
Matthew 20:26-28 (NIV)

I love my new truck. Well, at least it is new to me. It has a feature that caught me off guard. When I push a button, a lovely lady says to me, "Command, please." A person could really grow to enjoy that greeting. The lady in my truck wants to serve me. She wants to grant my every wish. If I want to change the radio, I just tell her. If I want to call someone, she does it for me. Wow, the world has not revolved around me like that since I was an infant. Could this really be true?

Most of us learned a long time ago that the world does not revolve around us. And I agree: it should not revolve around you, but what about me? Maybe you, like me, occasionally fall into the trap of thinking, "Life would certainly be better for everyone if the world revolved around me."

Infancy is a cruel start to life. We cry, and people respond to our needs. We smile, and people snap pictures. Others feed us and clean us. How sad that it quickly fades. Never again does the world say, "Command, please." While we may think we want to hear those words – "Command, please" – the truth is there is more satisfaction in serving than being served.

Greatness is revealed when the world does not revolve around us.

Look at our role model, Jesus. If anyone should have had the world revolve around him, it would have been Jesus. But scripture is clear: he did not come to be served. People around him did not say, "Command please." People did not cater to his every wish. In fact, the opposite was true. He served others and, by doing so, became the greatest one of all. His whole life was ministering to people. His life on earth concluded with his being the ultimate sacrifice for all of mankind.

Perhaps we should rethink how great it might be to be served and instead strive to be more like the son of man. Why not live a life in service to others? Why not give without expecting others to serve you? If you are a leader or a manager, why not seek to serve those who report to you? By helping them perform well, are you not, in fact, helping the organization to achieve optimal effectiveness? When you serve your family, are you not creating a better home life? Having a "serve others first" mindset is not only Christ-like, but savvy for those who want a great life.

The desire to have the world revolve around you, however, is a stubborn passion, so one day I thought I would test to see if my new truck had influenced those around me. I tested what I thought was my new reality in my truck when the lady asked me, "Command, please." I looked at my wife and told her she could learn from this lady. For some reason I felt a very sharp pain in my side. Ouch, well at least I still have my truck. And I have a purpose in life and the secret to greatness – to serve those who serve.

CHAPTER 39: FOUL WORDS

Do not let any unwholesome talk come out of your mouths, but only what is helpful to building others up and according to their needs, that it may benefit those who listen. Ephesians 4:29 (NIV)

... but no human being can tame the tongue. It is a restless evil, full of deadly poison. James 3:8

A preacher moved to a new neighborhood to start a new ministry. He unpacked an old bike that he had not ridden for years and took a ride on the bike to get to know his neighbors. Around one corner he noticed a man placing a "For Sale" sign on a lawn mower. He stopped, introduced himself, invited the man to come hear him preach, and then asked, "How much?" since he needed a new lawn mower.

"I haven't decided yet," the man answered. Since the preacher did not typically ride his bike, he asked, "Would you trade that lawn mower for this bike?" The man said, "Let me ride it first." So the preacher waited as the man took a brief spin on the bike. When he returned the preacher asks, "Do we have a deal?" "Yes, we do."

Then the preacher thought, I should probably crank this mower. As the man was riding away on his new bike, the preacher yelled, "The mower won't start." The man yelled back, "Yes it will, you have to cuss at it and kick it, but it will start."

"Sir, as I told you, I am a preacher. I do not cuss. I have walked with Jesus many years, and my old habits, such as cussing, are long gone." "Well preacher," the man said, "You just keep pulling on that cord to crank the mower. It will come back to you soon enough."

Sure enough, bad habits do come back with ease, even for the most mature Christians among us. That is why James was so bold to tell us that no one can tame the tongue. Even though we can tame many animals, for some reason the bad habit of using hateful language just seems to come back too often. Perhaps that is why Paul reminds us not to allow any unwholesome talk. All of our words should be encouraging those who hear them. Our listeners should not hear distasteful words.

What stressor causes you to want to use objectionable words? What is the task, event, or circumstance that makes you want to cuss? I am as human as the next person. For me, it is hanging curtains or drapes. For some reason I really hate doing this project. No one, not even a preacher, is immune from the dangers of the tongue.

But, is the world a better place when our words are wholesome? Would entertainment be just as good, or even better, without foul language? Are we perceived to be more intelligent when we avoid insalubrious words? Does unhealthy language harm us and those who hear our toxic words? Could politicians do a better job by addressing the issues rather than criticizing each other? Are the people we lead better off when our words are pleasant? And why do our children repeat only the words that we wished they had not heard?

While I do not remember cleaning my mouth out with soap when I was young, I do remember my mom threatening to do so, more than once. Now that I am old, I still need to keep all my words clean, just in case my mom can hear from Heaven. And because it is the right thing to do.

(Anecdotal Story)

CHAPTER 40: BABY STEPS | EASTER

He is not here; he has risen, just as he said. Come and see the place where he lay. Matthew 28:6 (NIV)

As we celebrate the Resurrection in our houses of worship, let's make sure we welcome all who attend, including those Christians who might overlook the fact that we have worship services each Sunday of the year. You know the type of Christians I am talking about. We sometimes call them "CE Christians" – you only see them in worship at Christmas or Easter or "submarine Christians" – resurfacing twice a year. Why do we Christians resort to devouring our own with such inappropriate words?

Yes, we know that we are not to stop meeting together as Christians (Hebrews 10:25). Gathering in weekly meetings with fellow believers is paramount to appropriate Christian development, helping us to study God's Word on a regular basis. Likewise, we are to meet regularly to worship, and in that worship we collectively celebrate and worship God. By being together, we strengthen our faith and grow and mature in our knowledge of God and His wonderful grace. All this is a part of normal spiritual growth. And, yes, we should spur one another on in these spiritual disciplines and even more as we get closer and closer to Christ's return. But growing in such grace and knowledge of God is not always typical.

Believers and followers of Jesus Christ, the Resurrected One, come in all stages of spiritual development. Some are still nursing on the milk of the Word. Some are ready to eat real food – even meat (1 Corinthians 3:2). So let's love and celebrate even baby steps of faith – even those we see in worship only on Christmas and Easter.

I have lived through something comparable with my own sons and grandchildren. Many of you have, too. You lovingly say to that one-year-old, "Touch your ear," and the darling begins to point to his or her nose and you gently redirect to the ear. And when our children finally touch their ears, we explode into applause as we celebrate the achievement of The Smartest Child ever in human history. We understand these baby steps, these tiny accomplishments. And we celebrate each one with great joy.

So regarding all those who come to our houses of worship this Easter – welcome them with love. Explode into applause and celebrate even the smallest baby steps of spiritual growth, even if it is something as simple as attending a worship service on Resurrection Sunday. It's a day to celebrate – as we do every Lord's Day – that He is not here. He is risen!

CHAPTER 41: TO TELL THE TRUTH

You shall not give false testimony. Exodus 20:16 (NIV)

Truth matters. It is not by mistake that speaking the truth makes it to the top ten in God's eyes. There was so much that God could have shared with his people as they were coming out of slavery in Egypt on their way to being free and self-governed. There were so many things they needed to know. Truth was among that Top Ten (Dennis Prager, *The Ten Commandments*).

For a people to survive on a macro or micro level, as a nation or as a family, truth is paramount. Truth must be valued above all else. Even the slightest contempt for truth could mean failure to an individual or to a nation. Truth is to be highly valued (Prager).

Think about it. Throughout history contempt for truth has been devastating. African slavery was based on the lie that blacks are inferior. Nazism was based on the lie that Jews are inferior. Communism and socialism are based on the misconception that government knows best (Prager).

Even today when we seek to fight a good fight, too often we hold truth too loosely. Homelessness numbers often are cited in the multi-millions. Yet the facts show that homelessness is closer to 500,000. Even if homelessness were in the mere hundreds, would it still not be worth our best efforts to try to reduce it? Those fundraising for breast cancer and other diseases have often cited exaggerated numbers. Why? (Prager) Disease needs to be eradicated. Much of the science behind global warming is actually junk science. This is sad because taking care of our planet is just savvy. We now know that "hands up, don't shoot" never happened. Even without that incident, we can still all agree that even one misjudgment by police or others in authority needs correction. Those advocating against domestic violence will often cite that there is a spike in such violence on Super Bowl Sunday. The problem is that it is not truth. But ending domestic violence, no matter what day it occurs on, or how many times, is paramount.

Even preachers are subject to this inane practice of overstating beyond truth. Some preachers cry that all drinking of alcohol is evil. Close, but the fact is that scripture condemns drunkenness (Proverbs 23:20, Romans 13:13, Galatians 5:21) and the bible speaks of appropriate use for a little wine (Psalm 104:15, 1 Timothy 5:23). While I understand why such overstatement occurs – alcoholism has been too close a friend amongst my family – it is not savvy. The end does not justify the means.

There is no lack of warning about truth telling (Exodus 23:1, Proverbs 19:9 and 25:18, Ephesians 4:25). While the ninth commandment is focused on speaking truth in the courts, most Hebrew scholars agree it is applicable to truth telling in general.

So as you conduct your affairs, in society or in the home, why not always speak the truth in love? (Ephesians 4:15) People deserve to hear the truth. But they deserve to hear truth surrounded by love. They do not need your arrogance and exaggeration. We should be kind, compassionate, and forgiving (Ephesians 4:32) in our communication of the truth.

While they were not directly from scripture, my mother's words reflected biblical truth and still echo in my head today: "Boy, if you cannot say anything nice, then bite your tongue. And if you can't tell the truth, be quiet." There are many times that I wished I had bitten my tongue. Many times I wish I would have swallowed blood rather than have had those words leave my mouth. Even when I was right, at times my self-righteousness was far from loving.

In all aspects of our lives truth is paramount. What would our society be like if politicians were always truthful? How different would it be if they actually kept their campaign promises? What if all businessmen were truthful? What would our family be like if we spoke truth and lived lives of integrity? When we are champions of a righteous cause, do we really need to weaken the validity of our cause by exaggerating numbers? Is not your cause valid enough? Do we want our spiritual leaders to speak when the bible speaks and be silent when the bible is silent? Would we all not benefit from truth?

(See *The Ten Commandments: Still the Best Moral Code*, by Dennis Prager, 2015, Regnery Publishing)

CHAPTER 42: COMMITMENT

So then, just as you received Christ Jesus as Lord, continue to live in him, rooted and built up in him, strengthened in the faith as you were taught, and overflowing with faithfulness. Colossians 2:6-7 (NIV)

Growing a pecan tree takes patience and a commitment to a long-term relationship. Depending on the variety of pecan tree, there will be no fruit for five to ten years, and a tree takes 20 or more years to fully mature.

Ten years ago I had visions of picking pecans from the trees in my yard. So I planted two trees. Let me just say – we will not have a pecan pie from the trees in my yard for years to come. But I am a very patient man. I am committed to long-term relationships. And I love pecan pie!

Growing in your faith takes patience and commitment, especially if you wish to share the sweetness of a strong faith with your great grandchildren. Solid roots in family, faith, and belief systems that survive the test of time and the struggles of life do not happen by chance. You must be intentional in habits that grow your faith. There must be a real commitment to long-term relationships.

A strong faith takes living in Him for years. For your faith to grow you must find yourself in Christ for more than just a day. Do you find yourself doing the things that would make Jesus smile every day? Do you give? Do you love? Do you grow in the grace and knowledge of your Lord Jesus Christ? Do you meet with other Christians to worship on a regular basis? Do you do those things with Him on a consistent basis week after week? Are you willing to give each and every year as Jesus would have you do? Are you living for Him and serving those around you over and over? As those days of living for Him turn into weeks, and those weeks turn into months, and those months into years, then your faith will be strong from living for Jesus.

A strong faith takes deep roots, roots that are attached to Him, the one who is life and hope and joy. Deep roots do not happen without effort. Deep roots allow one to weather all the storms of life on this side of heaven. Deep faith – the kind with deep roots – allows joy in the pain. Peace in the storm. Hope in the struggles. Strong roots of faith grow only over time as we trust in Him to do the work only He can do.

A strong faith takes years of teaching. Are we reading God's word? Are we meditating on scripture? Are we studying the Book? Are we listening to solid teaching and preaching? Are we memorizing verses from the Bible? And is it our goal not only to hear the Word but also to do what the Word says in our everyday life? Yes!

A strong faith takes time to develop just like those wonderful pecan trees. For now I will have to buy pecans for my wife to make her fantastic pecan pie. But one day my grandchildren will make pecan pies from pecans in Poppy's back yard. For now I will continue to walk every day in Him. Because patience and long-term commitments reap huge rewards . . . whether we are growing pecans or growing a strong and lasting faith.

CHAPTER 43: TRUTH WILL SET YOU FREE

Then you will know the truth, and the truth will set you free.
John 8:32 (NIV)

Question: If one decides to call a dog's tail a leg, then how many legs does a dog have? Before you answer this classic riddle, let's consider the reality about truth and how throughout history mankind has twisted words to try to twist truth.

Most people attribute this riddle to President Lincoln. Lincoln faced the flux of social norms similar to what we all face in our generation. Society standards have been, and will always be, in constant flux. When President Lincoln grew frustrated with the thorny issues of his time and the abuse of power to justify the inane pursuit to redefine truth, he is attributed to asking others this riddle. Actually, history clarifies in his riddle the animal of choice was a calf and not a dog. It is said Lincoln often smiled, for most people gave the wrong answer.

Funny thing about truth. Truth really does not care what you think. Truth does not ebb and flow with the change in society norms and standards. Truth does not care if it is popular. Truth is stubborn. Truth is consistent. Truth does not care if you curse at it. Truth does not get bothered even when the most esteemed among us rule against it. Truth does not get its feelings hurt. Truth is not intimidated. Truth is not always appreciated. Truth is not always valued. Truth is truth. It does not change. And with truth, there comes significant freedom.

We teach our children not to touch a hot stovetop or to put their hands in the fire. Why? Because they will get burned. No matter how much we want to rename hot or fire to cold. No matter how much we want to identify flames with ice, it does not work. Fire will burn, no matter what we call it.

When I was young, I lived with many mythical thoughts in my passion to twist truth. At one stage in my life I truly thought a Twinkie was food. It was the nutrition I needed to get through the day. Oh, how I wish that were true, but it is not. Now I am not saying a Twinkie is not delicious. I am saying that the truth is that a Twinkie has no nutritional value.

Now that I am not so young, I still lack the ability to change truth. My age has a stubborn way of not accepting my identifying myself as young. No matter how much I seek to identify with the college students that I serve – no matter how much I identify with their food choices, music choices, late nights, constant movement and activities – my body constantly reminds me I now have gray hair. Ugh, well at least I am beginning to get some cool senior discounts, even without asking!

Every generation should be very careful with truth. Is not seeking to twist truth dangerous? Should we allow our leaders to change truth? Should we allow big government and big business to redefine truth? Should we remind them and ourselves of Lincoln's riddle? And should we not smile when most give the wrong answer? There is freedom when we know truth.

So, if one decides to call a dog's tail a leg, then how many legs does a dog have?

CHAPTER 44: SHARING THE LIGHT

When Jesus spoke again to the people, he said, "I am the light of the world. Whoever follows me will never walk in darkness, but will have the light of life." John 8:12

In the same way, let your light shine before others, that they may see your good deeds and glorify your Father in heaven. Matthew 5:16 (NIV)

It is called the Centennial Light. It is a light bulb that has faithfully burned for 115 years. It was first installed in 1901. The Fire Department in Livermore, CA, has used this light bulb in multiple locations. This hand blown incandescent lamp with carbon filament was invented by Adolphe Chaillet, and was made by Shelby Electric Company. Currently it shines at 4 watts and serves as a night light over fire trucks. You can see the bulb on its web cam or visit the fire station. You can read books about this light bulb or view the numerous pictures of various celebrations.

There is another light. A light that has shined longer and brighter. This is a light that darkness cannot consume. This light reveals what is right and what is wrong. This light is for all people, not just for some. This light gives joy in times of pain. It is a light that guides our steps and our direction in life. And, if you follow this light, you will be all the better for your decision. Ultimately, there is salvation in this light. In this light, there is truth. In this light, there is hope. In this light, there is purpose. Life giving light.

This light is Jesus. He has always shined, and will always shine. He has called us out of darkness to shine for him. We are to point others to the light. We are to let our light shine so the world may see Jesus. It is not our primary role to point others to church. It is not our primary role to point others to a political party. It is not our primary role to convince people to right the wrongs of our time. It is our role to point people to the true light. And that light has a name. Jesus.

It is by the name of Jesus that people are saved. It is by the name of Jesus that people learn to live in harmony with others. It is by the name of Jesus that people learn the value of the local church, her fellowship and ministry. But let us be perfectly clear: it is Jesus that we present.

There is a song I sang as a little boy – "This little light of mine, I'm gonna let it shine." It was a whimsical song from my childhood that still reminds me I am to let everyone see God's light shining through me. So, is your light still shining? How many watts of light can others see? Do they know the light of Christ in your life? If not, why not?

CHAPTER 45: LIVING FAITH

As the body without the spirit is dead, so faith without deeds is dead. James 2:26 (NIV)

The family pet died. It happened while their son was at school. Mom, with every good intention, decided to dispose of the remains of the family cat before her son got home from school. This cat had been with her son since birth, and now the boy was in middle school. As soon as the son arrived home, as always, he looked for his cat.

Mom quickly intervened, "Son, I need to tell you – our cat died. Now, it is okay; he is in cat heaven."

"But, Mom," the son interrupted.

The mother was determined to share her best therapeutic lines: "The cat is better off." "Jesus is loving and petting the cat." "God loves all animals." But after each statement, the boy kept trying to interrupt. Finally Mom stopped and said, "What? What is your question?"

"Mom, what does God want with a dead cat?"

That is a good question: what does God want with a dead . . . faith? God has called us to be his hands and feet to the world around us. He has called us to do good deeds – acts of kindness as a demonstration of faith. We are to love people so that the world will see Jesus

Our works are not done to earn us salvation (Ephesians 2:8). We are not seeking a quid pro quo with our good deeds to gain a higher status with God. In fact, our best acts of goodness to a holy God can appear as filthy rags (Isaiah 64:6). After all, salvation is free, and grace is amazing.

Our works are a reaction to our position in Christ. We are saved by this amazing grace, so in celebration, we serve others. We do not serve to gain victory in Christ; we serve because we already have victory. It is our natural response to amazing grace.

How do you serve? Do you write cards of encouragement? Do you give of your time to tutor children? Do you donate books for children to read? When is the last time you reached out to a senior citizen, perhaps with yard work or a hot meal? Do you help those who come out of prison to get a fair and real chance to succeed in life? If you own a company, have you ever hired someone who has served time?

One of my sweetest memories is of a young man that I hired straight out of prison. He later came to me very awkwardly informing me that he had a better job offer, one that the company I owned could never offer him. I encouraged him to go to the new company only to have him protest, "But you took a chance on me." I asked him if he did a good job for me. We both knew that he had. Then I told him that all he owed me was a handshake and a smile. Now he was to help others, just as he had been helped. Those who can, should.

Indeed, God does not need our dead faith. We are to do something. There is no act of kindness that is too small. But in the doing, we must never forget that we are to do good deeds, not only for the sake of goodness, but also to point others to Jesus (Matthew 5:16, 1 Peter 2:12).

(Anecdotal Story)

CHAPTER 46: LET US WORSHIP

Come, let us bow down in worship, let us kneel before the Lord our Maker ... Psalm 95:6 (NIV)

It was the classic prearranged dinner for an older couple to meet with a younger couple for the purpose of mentoring. The young man was just so impressed by the older gentleman. How had he kept the love language alive, even after more than 50 years of marriage? Every response and request with his wife was so full of endearing terms like honey, my love, darling, sweetheart, pumpkin, etc. The two seemed to be so very much in love.

Toward the end of the evening, while their wives were out of the room, the young man just had to ask. "How have you kept the love alive? I think it's wonderful that after all the years you have been married, you still call your wife all those loving names."

The old man hung his head. "The truth is I forgot her name about ten years ago. That's why I use all those other words."

Sometimes I think we have forgotten God's name. I think we have forgotten that we, the Church, are the bride of Christ (Ephesians 5:23). We are to worship and adore our groom. We are to give him all the honor and glory. It is his name we are to remember. Our role is to worship him when we gather each week and, if he is lifted up, all men will be drawn to him (John 12:32).

Christ is the center of our worship. Worship has very little to do with us and everything to do with God. Have we forgotten what worship is all about? Has our relationship with Christ become so comfortable that we forgot his name years ago?

A recent church sign showed eight service options to serve the members: Classic Service 8 am, Contemporary Service 9 am, Mid Century Modern 10 am, Post Modern 11 am, Boomer Service noon, Millennials 1 pm, Blended Service 2 pm, and Happy Hour Service 4 pm. While I am sure the author was being facetious, it does point to a reality among us. Who are we serving – the worshipers, the seekers, the old guard, the new folks, or the one to be worshiped? The truth is, if we are focused on our style of worship, then we are missing the point. If we are still debating worship styles (traditional, contemporary, or modern), we are debating the wrong thing. Is this worship about lifting up Jesus? Is this about him, and his name?

No one should ever get stuck in any generation's favorite styles of music and worship. After all, we are told to admonish with psalms, hymns, and songs from the Spirit (Ephesians 5:19, Colossians 3:16). God has never requested the golden oldies. He has requested a new song (Psalm 33:3).

But, are we like the old man who forgot the name of his wife? Have we forgotten the name of our groom? Has our worship become habit? Do we know who the head of the church is? Do we know him by name? Is our relationship with him real and as fresh as the first day we called him Savior? Have we forgotten the purpose of worship? Do we remember why we come together each week?

(Anecdotal Story)

CHAPTER 47: BE A GIVER

"... see that you excel in this grace of giving." 2 Corinthians 8:7b (NIV)

I really like money. Hetty Green must have really loved money. Or at least it appears she did. During the Gilded Age in America, when women did not dominate in amassing wealth, she was known as the wealthiest woman in America, and at her death, likely the wealthiest woman in the world.

To say she was cheap would be an understatement. We are told she did not heat her oatmeal in the morning because it would cost money to do so. She wore only black and changed clothes only when they wore out. When she or family needed medical attention, she sought out free clinics for indigents. Some called her the "witch of wall street," and, a turn of the century phrase, "I'm not Hetty if I do look green" was attributed to her.[24]

Now, while I am sure that many of the stories about Henrietta Howland "Hetty" Green are urban legends, the truth is that she was a savvy woman – born with a silver spoon in her mouth, influenced by her faith, well versed in financial matters at a young age – who built and expanded the family business and rescued cities in financial trouble (at a profit, of course). Yet her stinginess was legendary.

---

[24] https://en.wikipedia.org/wiki/Hetty_Green

Wealth and stinginess do not have to be synonymous, but neither do poverty and stinginess. Christians, whether wealthy or poor or in between, are called to excel in the grace of giving (2 Corinthians 8:7). Even more, we are called to be cheerful givers (2 Corinthians 9:7). You can be a giver no matter how much wealth you have.

Common sense would tell us that if you are wealthy, you have the opportunity to impact others in big ways. Money does matter. Money can make a difference. Those with wealth have the opportunity, and perhaps the obligation, to make a significant difference for others through nonprofit groups and the churches they attend.

They say there are two types of people in the world: givers and takers. We all get to choose. Most will never have the wealth of Hetty Green, but we all can learn to give rather than cling to every dollar. In truth, most nonprofit organizations operate on $10-to-$100-dollar-a-month gifts. Churches operate with tithes from members. Your life will be fuller if you choose to be a giver. Give of your time to serve others. Give of your dollars to help others. Look for ways to share.

One word of caution to help us become givers: Beware – the love of money is the root of all kinds of evil (1 Timothy 6:10). The teachings of John Wesley can provide balance even for today's generation: "Gain all you can, save all you can, and give all you can."[25] How you deal with your money reveals what you truly love (Matthew 6:21).

Whether you are rich or poor, why not commit to live the rest of your life as a giver?

---

[25] http://www.umcmission.org/Find-Resources/John-Wesley-Sermons/Sermon-50-The-Use-of-Money

CHAPTER 48: GRADUATION

Be on your guard; stand firm in the faith; be people of courage; be strong. Do everything in love. 1 Corinthians 16:21 (NIV)

Special thanks to Northeastern High School, Elizabeth City, NC, for the privilege of speaking at their graduation. Go, Eagles! This column is adapted from that speech.

Congratulations graduates! I am reminded of a story about the great scientist Albert Einstein. Einstein was once traveling from Princeton on a train when the conductor came down the aisle, punching the tickets of every passenger. When he came to Einstein, Einstein reached in his vest pocket. He couldn't find his ticket, so he reached in his pants pocket. It wasn't there, so he looked in his briefcase but couldn't find it. Then he looked in the seat beside him. He still couldn't find it. The conductor said, "Dr. Einstein, I know who you are. We all know who you are. I'm sure you bought a ticket. Don't worry about it." Einstein nodded appreciatively. The conductor continued down the aisle punching tickets. As he was ready to move to the next passenger car, he turned around and saw the great Dr. Einstein down on his hands and knees looking under his seat for his ticket. The conductor rushed back and said, "Dr. Einstein, don't worry, I know who you are. No problem. You don't need a ticket. I'm sure you bought one." Einstein looked at him and said, "Young man, I too, know who I am. What I don't know is where I'm going."

Graduates need to know not only who you are, but where you are going.

Be on your guard. This world is full of people who will tell you what you cannot do. I am here to remind you, you can do anything! Guard your dreams. The first time I applied to a doctoral program, I was told, "No, you are not ready." The second time, I was told, "No, you are not the right color." The third time, I did not bother to finish the application. But the fourth time I applied, I was told, "Yes." As Dr. Perkins I urge you to guard your hopes for the future. Dream big. Do not listen to those who say you cannot, for you can.

Stand firm in the faith. Yes, you can talk about faith in the public sector. This great nation was founded on faith. The preamble of the Constitution of the State of North Carolina states: We, the people of the State of North Carolina, grateful to Almighty God, the Sovereign Ruler of the Nations, for the preservation of the American Union and the existence of our civil, political and religious liberties, and acknowledging our dependence upon Him for the continuance of those blessing to us and our prosperity, do, for the more certain security thereof and for the better government of this State, ordain and establish this Constitution. Never allow anyone, or any government, to take away your faith. The word was "of" not "from". We have freedom of religion, not freedom from religion. Your faith helps you to know who you are and where you are going.

Be people of courage; be strong. If no one has never told you, allow me. You are not special. Life will not revolve around you. Life is not fair, and can be downright ugly at times. It takes courage and strength to know who you are and where you are going. Remember the words of a great philosopher of my generation: "You've got to know when to hold 'em, know when to fold 'em, know when to walk away, know when to run." (Kenny Rogers)[26] It takes courage and strength to stand for your

[26] http://www.azlyrics.com/lyrics/kenyrogers/thegambler.html, accessed June 15, 2016 Kenny Rogers, "The Gambler," 1978

belief. It takes courage and strength to walk away. It takes courage and strength to know who you are and where you are going.

Do everything in love. Love is best expressed in our relationship with each other. Learn to celebrate the diversity found in humanity. America has been called a great melting pot. But I believe we are more like a stew pot – that humanity shines best, humanity loves best, when we celebrate the diversity found around the globe. When Momma made beef stew, those carrots were much better after being mixed with that meat. Those potatoes were great when they mixed with those onions. That meat was far better after stewing with those vegetables. Nevertheless, those carrots never became meat. And those potatoes never became onions. But because of the diversity in the pot ... yum, it sure was great. So do everything in love and learn to love everyone. Love helps us to know who we are and where we are going.

Be on your guard; stand firm in the faith; be people of courage; be strong. Do everything in love. If you do, you will know who you are and where you are going.

(Anecdotal Story)

CHAPTER 49: INTENTIONAL LIVING

… And let us run with perseverance the race marked out for us, fixing our eyes on Jesus … Hebrews 12:1b-2a (NIV)

The power of intentionality is amazing. I reflect back to the days when both of my sons were teens. Both were very good musicians, but one was amazing. I would overhear someone saying to one of them, "Man, I wish I could play an instrument like that." One son would often reply, "No, you don't." To which the protestor would respond, "Yes, I do." Then my son would ask, with youthful tact, "Are you willing to practice eight hours every day?" The response was often "No." Then my son would say, "Then you really don't want to play an instrument like that." It takes hours, every day, for years to become an amazing musician. Being focused does pay.

The writer of Hebrews talks about being focused. He challenges us to fix "our eyes on Jesus" (Hebrews 12:2a). The imagery is clear. Believers have a great cloud of witnesses that have already run the race of life in Christ and are cheering us on. So we cast off those things that hinder us from successfully running the race. We have to be intentional, every day, to avoid the sins that would trip us up. To do this, we focus forward, our eyes fixed on Jesus, the "pioneer and perfecter of faith" (Hebrews 12:2b). Living a Christian life in any culture is a focused life.

Being intentional has its reward, but it also comes at a high cost. The cost can be simply stated – focus. There are things you have to do daily, and there are things you must avoid daily. Researchers once told us that it takes doing something for 21 days before you have a habit, a discipline. Now they tell us it is more like 66 days. But the truth for believers is that we are to be faithful all the days of our life. (Revelation 2:10)

So, are you focused? Do you think about the right things (Philippians 4:8)? Things that are true, noble, right, pure, lovely, admirable, excellent, praiseworthy – these are worthy for our mind to ponder. Do you do the right things (James 1:22)? Knowing the right thing to do but not doing it has little value. The value is in doing. Is your lifestyle one of loving God and your neighbor? Will people recognize you as a true believer by your actions? Are you known as a kind and compassionate person?

Let's be intentional in doing the right thing all the time, whether or not it is appreciated or valued by others. The price of being a good Christian is high.

CHAPTER 50: INDEPENDENCE DAY

I have come that they may have life and have it to the full. John 10:10b (NIV)

"We hold these Truths to be self-evident, that all Men are created equal, that they are endowed by their Creator with certain unalienable Rights, that among these are Life, Liberty, and the Pursuit of Happiness" ... these words from the beginning of the second paragraph of the Declaration of Independence are core to what we celebrate as Americans on the 4th of July. Our nation is unique among all nations throughout history. Our nation was one of the first that placed the ultimate authority in the people, not in government. Our nation was one of the first to intentionally limit government. The government's power comes from the governed, the people. "It is the Right of the People to alter or to abolish" the government. It is the right of the people to practice their faith (First Amendment of the U.S. Constitution). This is worth fireworks, time with family and friends, good food, reflection, and prayer, as we revel in our freedom in this great nation.

Now, we must be careful not to equate being a Christian with being part of a nation founded on Christian principles. The words "American" and "Christian" are not synonymous. They are not interchangeable. But to deny that our nation was founded on Christian principles is disingenuous. And to deny that our nation is great, partly due to the ideas found in the words above (regarding government and the consent of the governed, that is, the people), would be insincere. America is special. Just travel abroad, and you will soon recognize how special this nation is and deepen your appreciation for the freedoms found in America.

Life, liberty, and the pursuit of happiness are embedded in the American culture. But there is a greater culture, a greater community – Christianity. In Christianity there is something greater: it is called "abundant life." This abundant life is available to those who give their lives to Christ. Jesus was clear – it is Satan that lies and seeks to destroy and take away your life. Satan wants to destroy your very soul and take away your freedoms in Christ.

In direct contrast, Jesus came to earth to give life. Jesus gives not a simple life, but a full life. When we follow his voice, we are safe from thieves and wolves who seek to destroy our lives. When we follow his voice, we are saved.

So on this holiday as you watch the fireworks, take a moment to thank God you live in a country that has no laws "prohibiting the free exercise" of your faith. May you have a full life with family and friends, thanking God for freedom to follow him, his voice, toward safety and peace.

CHAPTER 51: PEACE | RACISM

Blessed are the peace makers for they will be called the children of God. Matthew 5:9 (NIV)

Peace. Shalom. Panpi. Satta. Paz. Paix. No matter what language or culture, peace is commendable. Peace is easily eroded, hard to keep, but always worth our earnest efforts.

One of the roles of government is keeping the peace. Christians are urged to pray for civil leaders so that we may indeed live in peace (2 Timothy 2:1). One such leader is Dallas Police Chief Davis Brown. His remarkable leadership during the horrid 2016 murders of police officers in Dallas is commendable. But it is even more fascinating when you know part of the back story.[27] His very own son was killed by police officers, after being shot 12 times, after his son killed a police officer. His brother was murdered by drug dealers. If anyone deserves our attention on this subject of peace, it is Chief Brown. "We're hurting. Our profession is hurting. Dallas officers are hurting. We are heartbroken," Brown said. "There are no words to describe the atrocity that occurred to our city. All I know is this: This must stop, this divisiveness between our police and our citizens."

Indeed this must stop. Good people must never return violence with violence. Hate must never cause more hate. "Hate cannot drive out hate; only love can do that." (Martin Luther

---

[27] http://www.cnn.com/2016/07/09/us/dallas-police-chief-david-brown-profile/

King, Jr.)[28] Love is always the answer. Love can bring about peace. Hate and violence never will give us peace.

Would we, as a group, rather live in peace or in hate and violence? Can we not agree to disagree at times? Can we not examine or debate a concept or theory without devaluing a fellow human?

Whatever happened to respect for others? Whatever happened to due process of the law? Should we not wait for justice to be determined? Why do so many people thrive on keeping racism, controversy, and division alive?

Jesus is clear in his teachings, especially in the well-known "Sermon on the Mount." Hate is too much of a burden to bear. Hate gives birth to violence. And since violence is as harmful to the hater as it is to those they hate, the weight of hate is heavy. True contentment and happiness are found in being a peacemaker. Satisfaction is found in seeking to live in peace with everyone. It is easy to hate. It takes courage and determination to live in peace with others. Peace is complex. Peace is birthed out of love and respect for every tribe, every nation, and every people.

Join me in praying for peace. Join me in treating everyone with love and respect. Join me in striving for peace in every aspect of our lives. And when we do, we will be known as children of God.

---

[28] http://www.usatoday.com/story/news/nation-now/2016/01/15/10-twitter-martin-luther-king-jr-quotes-mlk-day/78836904/

CHAPTER 52: ACT JUSTLY

He has shown you, O mortal, what is good. And what does the Lord require of you? To act justly and to love mercy and to walk humbly with your God. Micah 6:8 (NIV)

The political season is upon us again. Many will ignore it until the last moment prior to voting. Some will disregard it and not vote at all. Some will consume it 24/7 until Election Day. Most of us fall somewhere between.

Savvy Christians will want to remember several important principles and ideas in this season.

First, God is not a Republican nor is He a Democrat. He does not belong to the Tea Party, Fair Tax movement, Libertarian Party, or any special interest group. God is sovereign (Psalm 140:7). He is above all nations (Daniel 7:14). Governments rest on His shoulders (Isaiah 9:6). Christ is above all cultures, all countries, all people. During this political season we should pray more, seeking God's plans for our nation and for all nations. God's plans are more important than any political party. God's plan is for humans to live in harmony with each other. God's plan is for peace for all mankind.

Second, we must be careful not to confuse the role of government with the role of the church. Too many Christians are saying, "I cannot vote for this candidate because he/she is . . . [fill in the blank – not spiritual enough, too sleazy, a liar, corrupt, etc.]. While these descriptions may apply, consider the differences between the role of government and the role of the church. We are not electing a minister. We are electing those to serve us in government. Now to be clear, a Godly man or woman is preferred in government, but such a choice is not always one we have in candidates (Romans 13:1-8). Should we refrain from voting if we have a less-than-stellar choice for a candidate? Certainly not. God has historically used both men and women, good and bad, to move the nations to fulfill his will. God's providence in human history is often unclear to mortal man, even the most erudite. But we can seek to vote for the best from among the choices before us. We can pray for our governmental leaders. We can respect authority. We can and should be actively involved in the process.

Third, to do our part for a good society, the rules for Christians do not change whether we are governed by true believers or by those who are not.

1. Act justly. Justice is for everyone regardless of economic status, skin pigmentation, heritage, etc.

2. Love mercy. People are human, and they make mistakes. When they do so, we are to desire mercy for our fellowman because it is likely we will need mercy ourselves very soon.

3. Walk humbly with God. God is in charge. God rules the nations. God ordains whom He chooses to govern, so submit to him. Every day do the things that He would have you to do, and say the things that He would have you to say.

So think. Pray. Ponder whom you will vote for. Strive to live in harmony by listening more and talking less. We are to be God's people, even during the political season. Rest in Christ, not in politics. Even we mortals have a role to play in politics.

CHAPTER 53: PERVERT

Marriage should be honored by all, and the marriage bed kept pure, for God will judge the adulterer and all the sexually immoral. Hebrews 13:4 (NIV)

Pervert. Can we even use this word anymore? Please do not get mad at me. I am just asking a question. Pervert as defined by Google is "a person whose sexual behavior is regarded as abnormal or unacceptable – synonyms: deviant, degenerate."[29]

We find ourselves having some interesting debates today in America about sex, marriage, and one-flesh union. Christians in America and around the globe have always lived in a pluralistic society. We understand that many around us will not uphold what God's Word has to say about purity and sexuality. And among Christians there is not always agreement on Biblical standards for sexuality. Also, believers understand that many around us will call evil good and good evil, as referenced in Isaiah 5:20. Indeed, even Christians often struggle with keeping their sexual relationships in line with God's law, just as they might struggle with other sins, such as greed, jealousy, and lying. Christians, in fact, are simply sinners saved by grace. As such, they sometimes pervert healthy sexuality defined in God's

---

[29] https://www.google.com/webhp?sourceid=chrome-instant&ion=1&espv=2&ie=UTF-8#q=Pervert

Word. (Ugh – I used the word "pervert" as a verb; well, we have not banned the word yet.)

But has the world around us gone mad? Has society lost all common sense?

Did you know that many credible dictionary sources are adding an abundance of choices to gender identities?[30] Others have lists that include over 50 different genders.[31] We used to have two: male and female (Genesis 1:27b). Now, please do not extrapolate more than I am asking. Everyone, regardless of lifestyle, is a child of God, our creator. Everyone is to be respected and loved. Everyone should have the right to live life in peace.

But my question remains. Are we, as a people, seeking to delete the word "pervert"? Is anything considered sexually immoral anymore? Should we delete the word pervert? In our efforts to be inclusive, are we destroying a good society? Will there be any standards going forward? If so, who will decide? And by what standard will healthy sexuality be defined?

As one considers these questions, I was amazed at a recent promo for a new show using the tag line: "suspense, drama, and plenty of perverted sex". Ugh, so there is perversion?!?

The history of America is that of a country based on Judeo-Christian values that allowed for people to live freely among each other regardless of their personal belief system, with few exceptions. A person could indeed have no belief in God whatsoever. Everyone could live in peace and allow others to live and let live. But now we seem to have made Christianity and other faiths the enemy. With the good intention of trying to make sure everyone feels loved and included, have we swung the pendulum so far that we soon will have no standard of morality, especially in the area of human sexuality? Just asking.

---

[30] http://abcnews.go.com/US/merriam-webster-adds-genderqueer-genderfluid-gender-neutral-title/story?id=38675250

[31] http://abcnews.go.com/blogs/headlines/2014/02/heres-a-list-of-58-gender-options-for-facebook-users/

While we wait for the answer to the question, "Will the word 'pervert' become antiquated, be eschewed as hate speech, and be banned by all good inclusive people," please follow God's advice: let us love all those around us regardless of their preferences even as we continue to hold fast to the ancient words of truth.

CHAPTER 54: BARBARIANS VS. PEACE

There is a time for everything, and a season for every activity under the heavens: ... a time for war and a time for peace.
Ecclesiastes 3:1, 8b (NIV)

Barbarians are at the gate. When we hear of tragedy, around the globe or down the street, one of our first instincts is to ask, "Was this another terror attack?" And no wonder. A recently published analysis has revealed that in the years 2002 to 2015 there have been 4,900 terrorist events globally by these extremists, and 33,000 people have died as a result of this evil.[32]

These barbarians have called themselves Taliban, Al-Qaida, Hezbollah, ISIL, ISIS, Hamas, Boko Haram, Daesh, etc. They are extreme terrorists, bent on imposing their perverted religion on the entire globe in a holy Jihad. They seek a Caliphate, and they claim absolute authority over all Muslims and humanity. This struggle is beyond barbaric. The beheadings, the rapes, the slavery, the killing of those with alternative lifestyles, the burnings, the drownings, the mass murders, and more flood our news headlines far too often.

So what are we to do as a good society?

How should a Christian react?

---

[32] http://freebeacon.com/national-security/isis-affiliates-killed-33000-people-since-2002/

I do not presume to understand global politics, nor do I wish to enter that debate. Instead, I offer you some spiritual truths to consider to guide you during these troubling times.

Pray for peace. Just as David called for prayers for peace for Jerusalem (Psalms 122:6), everyone should pray for peace for all cities. We should seek peace. We should seek God's intervention among the nations so that all people can live in peace.

Do not fear. God is greater. God will provide a way. The one whom we worship is greater than anything in this world (1 John 4:4). We should continue to live our lives serving God by serving others.

Pray for government leaders. One of the clear rolls of government is to provide peace so that we can live quiet lives (1 Timothy 2:1-2), so that we can live our lives in godliness and holiness. Regularly ask God to protect our leaders and grant them wisdom as they seek to serve and protect us. Pray that they will not declare war swiftly and, conversely, that they will not delay in declaration of war when unavoidable, as it is hard to reason with those who are so barbaric.

Pray for Jesus to be known. Pray for the salvation of all people. Pray for those, even as you read this column, who seek to minister to those who desire to do so much harm to others. May those who seek evil be converted to seek good. May they come to know the One who will give them peace.

There is more advice that could be given to guide us as we live in the shadow of deep evil, but it may be helpful to remember that living in troubled times is not unique to our generation. In fact, from a historical perspective, times have been worse. But these are, indeed, troubling times when one considers the threat of global terrorist extremism. God is faithful and will guide us and our leaders during these days. Seek peace. Seek God. And point everyone to the author and creator of peace. So that we can live at peace with every tribe and every nation. For every tribe and every nation belong to God.

CHAPTER 55: LIFE AND DEATH

There is a time for everything, and a season for every activity under the heavens: a time to be born and a time to die, ...
Ecclesiastes 3:1-2a (NIV)

The doctors asked her for a private meeting about her husband's health. Her husband waited anxiously. Privately, the doctor described the severity of the situation to the wife. But he gave hope. Her husband could die soon, or he could have several more good years. But all stress has to be removed from his life. Food has to be fresh and healthy. Arguing is to be eliminated. Home life should be peaceful. Regular intimacy is a must. Her role would be to create for her husband the best of healthy living. She listened but made no comment. She pondered the physician's words as she walked out in silence. When her husband saw her, he quickly asked, "What did the doctor say?" "Honey," the wife replied gently, "you will die soon."

Death. None of us can avoid it. While this fictional story makes us laugh, those are true words: you will die. The only question is when. All of us will die, or we will see the Lord's return. Even those whom Jesus raised from the dead died (again) eventually. So accepting that we humans have a 100% mortality rate, let's reflect on some truths.

Live life on this side of heaven to the fullest. God has given us abundant life (John 10:10), so live your life in service to others and to God. Enjoy every moment with family and friends.

Do things you love with people you love. Serve God by looking for ways to help others. Help others with no expectation or possibility of pay back. When you do, not only will those you help be blessed, but also you will be what God wants you to be.

Seek peace. It is so important to "live in peace with each other" (Thessalonians 5:13b). Life is complex, chaotic, cruel, and unfair. So learn to forgive. Even when you are right and the others are wrong. Forgiveness and peace are partners in becoming who God has called us to be. Life is far too short not to live in peace. Life is far too short to hold on to pain. If you have not spoken to someone in years because of a past hurt, let it go, forgive, and live in peace.

God loves you. His desire is not for you to perish (2 Peter 3:9), but rather to have everlasting life with Him (John 3:16). So make peace with God. Be born of the water and of the Spirit (John 3:5). Follow the instructions Peter gave when he was asked, "What shall we do?" to be saved (Acts 2:37-38). No one is promised tomorrow. Be ready to stand before God. Today.

I hope that you will live a long and prosperous life. I pray you are ready to meet God. Do not fear death. Seek peace. The best life is yet to come.

(Anecdotal Story)

CHAPTER 56: THE WAY TO SALVATION

Jesus answered, "I am the way and the truth and the life. No one comes to the Father except through me. John 14:6 (NIV)

A new doctor in town posted an ad advertising his new practice. But one good ol' boy saw it as an opportunity to outwit the erudite. The ad read: "I can cure anything for $500 cash. No insurance. If not, I will give your $500 back plus another $500. Cash only." So, the good ol' boy decided this would be an easy way to make $500.

The man made an appointment and paid his $500 to the clerk. In the examination room he told the educated doctor he had lost all taste. The physician did a typical examination and tried several medical procedures to no avail. His patient, no matter how bitter, sour, or sweet, claimed he had no taste. The man was smiling. But then the doctor told his nurse to go to the back room, pour four ounces from a certain container, and bring him the glass of liquid. He then told his patient to drink the entire contents of the glass. As soon as it touched his lips, he spat it out, saying, "Doc, are you trying to kill me? That is kerosene." The doctor replied, "You are cured. You have your taste back." The good ol' boy left the office.

A month later he returned, thinking he now had an ailment that the doctor certainly could not cure. This time he would stump the doctor. He paid again. "Doctor, I have lost my memory." The doctor administered several procedures and a memory test, but his patient failed them all. He called his nurse in, he asked her if she remembered this patient from his last visit. She affirmed she did. He then instructed her to go get four ounces of the same liquid from the back. Immediately the man protested, "Doc, are you trying to kill me again? That is kerosene." The doctor replied, "You are cured. You have your memory back." The good ol' boy left the office.

Another month later he returned, knowing that this time he certainly had an ailment the doctor could not cure. He paid again. "Doctor, I cannot see." After careful examination and several failed procedures, the doctor conceded that he could not cure the man's blindness. So he told him he was very sorry and that indeed he would get his money back, plus an additional $500. So he starting placing $100 bills in his hand and counted, "One hundred, two hundred, three . . . ." "Wait, wait, those are not one-hundred dollar bills. Those are one dollar bills," protested the man. "You are cured. You have your sight back." The good ol' boy left the office.

At times, we are just like the man in this story: we think we can outwit God. Why do we try so many ways to find God? Why do we think there are so many paths to heaven? Why do we believe it does not matter which path we follow, in spite of the fact that he has given us instructions?

Some try bargaining with God. "God, I'm not so bad." We claim to be without sin. Well, at least without any major sin. But that thought is not consistent with scripture that reminds us that we are all sinners (Romans 3:23) and that the penalty for sin is death (Romans 6:23).

Others seek to persuade God by showing that they do good deeds. "Look at all the good I do for my fellowman. Certainly my acts of righteousness get me into heaven." Perhaps you have heard this said at a funeral: "Well, if anyone makes it to heaven, she will. She was such a good person." The problem is, according to the prophet Isaiah, our righteous acts are like filthy rags to a holy God (Isaiah 64:6).

So we cannot claim to be without sin or to be righteous in our lifestyle. We cannot hide our sins from God or brag about our righteousness. But why try, don't we? Do we really think we can outwit God? Why not simply accept his plan? He provides salvation in His Son, Jesus. Salvation is a gift from God, a wonderful plan found only in His son.

(Anecdotal Story)

CHAPTER 57: RULE OF LAW

But let justice roll on like a river, righteousness like a never-failing stream! Amos 5:24 (NIV)

Which is better, "rule of man" or "rule of law"? This is a valid question. Be very careful you understand all the implications before you answer. So much of our potential to live in peace rests on society's knowing the difference and the willingness to implement the correct choice. This country was founded in part as a revolt against the rule of man. It was thought that a rule of law was superior.

One of my favorite books of the Old Testament is Amos. But the context of his generation was shameful, at best. People were divided. There were ten tribes in the north called Israel. There were two tribes down south called Judah. Social injustice and lack of understanding the importance of God was as common as sunshine. In their relationships with each other, the poor were being neglected. In the marketplace, the scales were tilted. The court systems were deeply corrupt. (Amos 2:4-8) In their relationships with God, their faith was very weak, if not dead. Ceremonialism took over the worship service, the worship itself was poor, they bragged about tithes and free will offerings, and they wanted the "day of the Lord" to come (Amos 5:18-23). There was no reverent fear of God. God was irrelevant. Sound familiar?

God had sent Obadiah to help out, to no avail. God had sent Joel to make improvements, to no avail. In the midst of all this, God sent Amos – who was a shepherd and a farmer – to call his people back to him since they would not listen to his prophets. And it was in the midst of his message that Amos cries, "But let justice roll on like a river, righteousness like a never-failing stream!"

Perhaps that message is needed again today for our great nation. We need to return to the authority of the law, not the authority of man.

The rule of law allows justice. The rule of man will always eventually tilt toward injustice. When men and women rise to power – unless the rule of law applies to them the same as it does to those without power – there will eventually be abuse. Some leaders are often well-intended dragons. In the words of one of our founding fathers, John Adams, "Power always thinks it has a great soul and vast views beyond the comprehension of the weak; and that it is doing God's service when it is violating all his laws."[33]

Indeed, people – even our leaders – intend to do good. But is it not imperative that they, too, be subject to the law? Is justice not blind to position, power, wealth, fame? If the law does not apply to all, then will not some suffer? If the rule of man is considered superior to the rule of law, are we not doomed?

May we all understand the importance of the "rule of law' in contrast to the "rule of man" and the significance of the differences between the two. May our conscience be guided by a faith in God since "Our Constitution was made only for a moral and religious people. It is wholly inadequate to the government of any other" (John Adams).[34]

---

[33] http://www.john-adams-heritage.com/quotes/

[34] http://www.john-adams-heritage.com/quotes/

CHAPTER 58: RESTORATION | FORGIVENESS

"Come now, let us settle the matter," says the Lord. "Though your sins are like scarlet, they shall be as white as snow; though they are red like crimson, they shall be like wool." Isaiah 1:18 (NIV)

Pottery is beautiful. Throughout history, handcrafted pottery tells the story of functionality and works of fine art. Archeologists can give accounts of civilizations that have come and gone from pottery uncovered. There is one practice in pottery that tells an amazing story: kintsugi.

Kintsugi is the craft of repairing broken pottery with gold. A story has been handed down of a Japanese shogun, Ashikaga Yoshimasa, who was not pleased with repairs done to a piece of pottery he had sent back to China for repairs. So his own craftsmen set out to use precious metal to make repairs, actually accenting the brokenness instead of trying to hide the flaws. It seems the resulting beauty made kintsugi so popular that some would actually break their pottery just to have it repaired by masters in kintsugi. Whether these stories are true or not, many fine art galleries today will feature the craft of kintsugi, broken pottery with flaws that are not hidden, but instead accented with fine gold and other precious metals such as silver or platinum and more.

Broken pottery treated in this way tells the story of a brokenness that is not to be disregarded, but rather embraced and held by the master craftsmen. To many, the restored pottery is even more beautiful than the original, unbroken vessel.

Each of us is a sinner, according to Romans 3:23. Our lives are broken by our sins. We bring to God nothing of value. As a nation and as individuals we have broken His laws and rebelled against him in both simple and complex ways. We are broken pieces of humanity.

Isaiah sought to call God's people from brokenness to restoration. The call was for the nation to wash and clean up, to stop doing what was wrong, and to do right, seek justice, end oppression of others, and care for the fatherless and the widows (Isaiah 1:16-17). Is this not what is needed today?

God is an amazing craftsman. He does amazing work. As a nation, we should allow him to heal our land and put us on a path of peace with respect for all people. As individuals, we should allow him to heal our brokenness with the loving sacrifice of his son, Jesus. Restored lives can be more beautiful than ever. And restored lives are even more beautiful than restored pottery. While pottery is restored with precious metals, humans are restored by the precious blood of the lamb.

Is it not time to settle this matter, as Isaiah said? Would you like to be restored? You can be even more beautiful than ever.

CHAPTER 59: RESPECT YOUR VOTE

Let everyone be subject to the governing authorities, for there is no authority except that which God has established. The authorities that exist have been established by God. Romans 13:1 (NIV)

Clinton. Trump. Johnson. Stein. Each of us had the opportunity to go to the polls and vote for one of the four individuals running for President in 2016. Voting is your privilege and should not be taken for granted.

The 2016 election season appeared to be rife with contention, contention that is evident in various forms of social media, such as, but not limited to, Facebook and Twitter. We need to be careful that our passion for one particular candidate, or our passion against one particular candidate, does not put us at odds against each other, especially our brothers and sisters in Christ. Your passion, or lack thereof, should not cause lingering tension among family, friends, and co-workers.

Some people choose to be very private about whom they plan to vote for. Others are very public with their preferences. Please respect both choices. For years I have chosen to be public with my choices because others often ask me sincerely for advice. I do not recall telling people whom to vote for. I do recall telling people whom I am voting for and why, allowing them to make their own decision. But this voting cycle appears to cause deep frustration among many who are struggling with knowing, or not knowing, whom to vote for. Why?

Perhaps we need to revisit some advice from the preacher John Wesley on elections: "I met those of our society who had votes in the ensuing election, and advised them. 1. To vote, without fee or reward, for the person they judged most worthy; 2. To speak no evil of the person they voted against; and, 3. To take care their spirits were not sharpened against those that voted on the other side." [35] These words are as relevant today as they were when spoken in the seventeen hundreds.

Many are frustrated with politics. They perceive the etymology of the word "politics" is too close for comfort: "poly" meaning many and "tics," a blood-sucking animal. Sarcasm abounds with another phrase: "vote early – vote often."

But let's be very careful.

The bedrock of this nation is the privilege of voting. Respect one another's choices, especially when they conflict. Be civil. Have genuine discussion and even debate, if so desired, with both parties. But when you are done with your discussion in private or public, or in social media, whether you agree on who should be the next President of these United States or not – respect each other and thank God for the privilege of freedom.

Biblical truths remind us of the magnitude of voting and other processes in society. Governments are established by God. (Romans 13:1) Government is on God's shoulders. (Isaiah 9:6) We should we pray for leaders in government. The role of government is to provide peaceful lives for her citizens. (1 Timothy 2:1, 2) Indeed this is serious, but we do not need to be disrespectful.

So, I would add to Wesley's charge to remind you to pray about your decision. Think about who, among the choices,

---

[35]

https://books.google.com/books?id=vKw0AQAAMAAJ&pg=PA29&lpg=PA29&dq=john+wesley+i+met+those+of+our+society+election&source=bl&ots=9IvloUK9hx&sig=TM2I9o sQO4yhG8_OEQ4WssUJC5o&hl=en&sa=X&ei=1EqAUJiAG-yhyAG2uoDAAQ#v=onepage&q=john%20wesley%20i%20met%20those%20of%20our%20society%20election&f=false

would best represent you and your values that have been shaped by God's word. Rarely will anyone be an ideal candidate. Peace as you head to the polls to vote.

CHAPTER 60: DYSFUNCTION AND GRACE

But God demonstrates his own love for us in this: While we were still sinners, Christ died for us. Romans 5:8 (NIV)

God has a long history of working through people who come from dysfunctional families. After all, a dysfunctional family is any family with more than one person in it (Karr).[36] And every human is a sinner (Romans 3:23). So when two or more sinful people form a family, it is not uncommon for the family to be dysfunctional on more than one level. And out of that chaos comes God's story.

Too many still think that the Bible is full of perfect people who lived perfect lives in perfect families, and that we are failures and God cannot use us unless we and our families are perfect. For many, the first time they really read the Bible they are surprised by all the stories of people from dysfunctional families that are used by God. In fact, they soon realize when they read the Bible for themselves, with genuine open hearts and minds, that it might even be difficult to find that perfect family in God's Word. The Bible is not full of people with glowing halos that do the right thing every time and in every situation. The people in the Bible are normal people with messed up lives and dysfunctional families.

---

[36] Mary Karr, *The Liar's Club,* Penguin Books

Look at the first family, for example – Adam and Eve and their sons. In their family, one son, Cain, killed the other son, Abel (Genesis 4:8). Imagine the dysfunction this caused. And later, what about the brothers Jacob and Esau? Jacob swindled Esau out of his birthright with bread and stew, since Esau despised his birthright (Genesis 25:29-34). Talk about tension between brothers. Look at Joseph – his brothers wanted to kill him because they were so jealous of him and the favor their father showered on him. One brother talked the others out of murdering Joseph, but they faked his death and sold Joseph into slavery (Genesis 37:18-36). And these are just three examples within the first couple of generations of God's people. The Bible is full of these stories from beginning to end. Yet, when we read about these families, we see evidence of God's loving patience in working with us to help us find peace in our families.

All of a sudden I am so thankful for the relationships I have with my seven siblings. And I am thankful for the relationship that my own sons have with each other. While chaos abounds in my large family tree, I have no memory of anything close to what we read about in these families in God's word.

Families are complex and dysfunction ensues when we, or our families, lose focus on God. Restoration out of dysfunction happens when we begin to do things God's way. God wants us to live in peace within our families and with our fellow man. You may come from a fairly normal family, or your family history may be totally crazy. Either way, read on.

Jesus is not afraid of your dysfunctional family. Jesus is not afraid of your idiocy. He works through ordinary people from ordinary families full of chaos, pain, failure, and triumph. God loves us and offers us healing in the midst of our foolishness. The great news is that God loves you before you get your act together. No matter how crazy your life or family tree is, God has said, in so many words, "I want to use you. I want you to be part of my plan for healing and peace. Your history of pain and chaos can help others find peace and healing." God wants to use you to help others.

So are you convinced yet? Are you ready to help others, even though your past is not perfect? Are you willing to allow something good to come out of your dysfunction? Isn't it time to end the insanity and help others? Do you recognize that dysfunction comes from not doing things God's way? Think about it.

When we read the Bible we find that God does amazing things with normal people. And he is still doing extraordinary things with people like you and me.

CHAPTER 61: UGLY RACISM

For God so loved the world that he gave his one and only Son, that whoever believes in him shall not perish but have eternal life. John 3:16 (NIV)

Are you as tired of racism as I am?

Racism is idiocy. Racism is inane. Racism is senseless. Racism is thoughtless. Racism is futile. Racism is absurd. Racism is reckless. Racism is irresponsible. Racism is damaging. Racism is ridiculous. Racism is wickedness. Racism is iniquity. Racism is evil. Racism is immoral. Racism is wrong. Racism is offensive. Racism is misbehavior. Racism is perverted. Racism is infringement. Racism is intolerance. Racism is disruption. Racism is sin.

Racism has no place in any society and especially not in the church. Racism should never be in the in heart or lifestyle of those who choose to follow Christ.

Let me be plain spoken. Those who make a decision about other human beings merely on the basis of their skin pigmentation are doing so because someone has taught them to do so. Sadly, some have handed down to others the misconception that some people are better than others based on skin color. I wonder if at some point someone thought this was a good idea and that it would work. But it never was and never has. The practice of separating the races has never benefited society. It degrades society instead.

It is time to stop. It is time to get over this sickening trend. There is no "racism gene." We are not born bigots, rather we learn bigotry's hateful characteristics. The reversing of racism comes when we unlearn bigotry and accept the truth that there is only one race. The human race. "God so loved the world . . . ." His son Jesus made this clear long ago on the cross. Jesus died for red, yellow, black, and white. Jesus loves. Jesus saves.

Our society needs to deal with racism now. Today. Thinking that we are better or worse than someone else, based on the amount of pigmentation in our skin, is illogical, at best. Pigmentation has nothing to do with our worth as a human being. It is time for racism to end.

Have we come so far in race relations only to reverse and go backward? Why does the race protest industry never stop disrupting society? When will we learn to listen to each other and enjoy our diversity? Why do we have a society in which so many can make an extraordinary living on keeping racism alive? Why is it that some communities in America respond with peace and prayers and others respond with hate and riots when racism rears its ugly head?

Will we ever learn to love one another?

CHAPTER 62: SWEET CONTENTMENT

I know what it is to be in need, and I know what it is to have plenty. I have learned the secret of being content in any and every situation, whether well fed or hungry, whether living in plenty or in want. Philippians 4:12 (NIV)

It might be hard for my friends to believe, but I was not always a perfect child. I know it is tough to imagine, but for the sake of the column, please do. Here's one example of less-than-perfect that occurred when I was a child, exact age forgotten.

My family was on the boardwalk at Myrtle Beach when I saw "The Holy Grail." It was large, it was sugar, and I needed to have that cotton candy Holy Grail. I had already had supper and ice cream, but that was not important to me. I clearly remember throwing a royal fit in a royal way. In retrospect, I realize that had my own child done this, he might have become fish bait. Indeed, that boardwalk was just a few steps from the waves of the Atlantic Ocean.

My parents reasoned with me the best that they could, saying things like, "Son, there is no possible way you can eat that." "Wait till next time." A few exchanges later, I knew I had won when these words were spoken, "Now if we buy this you have to eat it all." I had won the fight for the Holy Grail. I got what I needed. One more time I heard those words of victory, but this time it came with a twist, "O.K., we will buy that cotton candy but are you sure that you can eat it all?" Absolutely. Positively. No doubt I will, I will. My bold tantrum had won. I was holding a bag of what I needed: fluffy pure sugar known as cotton candy. And it was so big. So, so big. It was so big that, you guessed it, I couldn't eat it all.

To this day I do not like cotton candy. To this day I am reminded that there is a big difference between needs and wants. That was the lesson my parents taught me that day with the sugary cotton candy prize: there is a significant difference between a need and a want.

Being content in life is a valuable prize. Contentment allows you peace whether you are wealthy or poor. Many of you were born with a silver spoon in your mouth, while many were born with a plastic spoon. Surprisingly, contentment is equally difficult whether you started with silver or plastic. Contentment is accepting God's provision in your life. Simply stated, if we have food and clothing (1 Timothy 6:8), should we not be content? Who brought anything into this world and who can take anything out (1 Timothy 6:7)?

I recognize that living out the difference between needs and wants can become complex. Once I needed a pickup truck while my wife wanted a convertible. I recognize we have to balance this dilemma in life so that we can serve one another. I also recognize that those of us who try to do everything as if we are working for the Lord (Colossians 3:23) must take care not to call "contentment" what is actually lack of ambition or even laziness.

If you are able to learn the difference between a need and a want, then you will be a step closer to the prize of living a contented life. That kind of life will help you find peace during times of both plenty and scarcity. I trust you will not have to give up cotton candy to find contentment and peace.

CHAPTER 63: PRAY AND VOTE

I urge, then, first of all, that petitions, prayers, intercession and thanksgiving be made for all people – for kings and all those in authority, that we may live peaceful and quiet lives in all godliness and holiness. This is good, and pleases God our Savior . . . . 1 Timothy 2:1-3 (NIV)

It is so disappointing and disheartening to follow Christian conversation over the current election, especially on the Presidential level. Many of the conversations I have seen are absolutely inappropriate – one believer making the claim that no real Christian would vote for this candidate or that candidate. Since when has the Christian vote been monolithic? Christians have always voted on both sides of the aisle. Through the years, even my wife and I have at times have not voted for the same candidate. So as we prepare to go vote – or even if you have already voted – let's remind ourselves of some extant biblical principles and remind ourselves that our hope is in God and not in politics.

You can look all you want, but you will not find any moral prerequisites in the bible for governmental leaders. And the reality is, considering the two front runners in this year's presidential election – one of whom will be president – we are way beyond being able to rely solely on moral character rooted in biblical principles as our guide for choosing. Of course character matters. However, character alone is not our deciding factor. Our choice is direction.

The world may wish for us not to mix politics and religion, but that is not biblical. Throughout the bible God often mixes these two subjects. God has much to say about kings and governments. In fact, government is God's idea. God calls for his people to be subject to human government and reminds us that there is no authority/government that He did not establish (Romans 13:1-2).

In a country like America, Christians should vote based on guidance from biblical values. Vote for the candidates whose party platform you find in harmony with your values as those values have been shaped by the grace and knowledge of God. "It cannot be emphasized too strongly or too often that this great nation was founded, not by religionists, but by Christians; not on religions, but on the gospel of Jesus Christ. For this very reason peoples of other faiths have been afforded asylum, prosperity, and freedom of worship here." (Patrick Henry of Virginia) [37]Our votes should continue this great tradition.

Consider candidates that understand the biblical responsibility of government to her people. As our Declaration of Independence states: "We hold these truths to be self-evident, that all men are created equal, that they are endowed by their Creator with certain unalienable Rights, that among these are Life, Liberty and the pursuit of Happiness." Government is made to protect us so that we can live quiet and peaceful lives (1 Timothy 2:1-3). Government is to punish those who do wrong (1 Peter 2:13-14).

So, go vote. Think and pray before you vote. With rights – such as voting – and freedom found in this country, come great responsibilities. And may we, whether our candidates win or lose in the upcoming election, pray for all government leaders, both local and national. Pray that they will understand they are God's instruments to fulfill His role for government. Pray for this great nation. The only hope for America is God – not any political system or party.

---

[37] M. E. Bradford, *The Trumpet Voice of Freedom: Patrick Henry of Virginia*, Plymouth Rock Foundation

CHAPTER 64: THE PURPOSE OF WEALTH

... Well done, good and faithful servant! You have been faithful with a few things; I will put you in charge of many things, Come and share your master's happiness! Matthew 25:21b (NIV)

It is an odd question for the son of a truck driver, who was the son of a share cropper, to ask, but the question is valid: What is the purpose of wealth? I understand there is a deceptive presupposition that anyone who creates wealth is evil. This mindset comes from passages like "the love of money is a root of all kinds of evil" (1 Timothy 6:10), which is true. But the same book presents the wealthy man as the hero in the parable of the talents (Matthew 25:14-30). And we are reminded in Proverbs 13:22 that a "good man leaves an inheritance for their children's children." "Indeed the Jewish tradition views a person's quest for profit and wealth to be inherently moral" (Rabbi Lapin).[38]

Somehow most Judeo-Christians do not have such a noble view of wealth creation. Indeed, many Christians see wealth creation as inherently depraved. Perhaps that needs to change, since if one considers wealth creation to be morally reprehensible, then making money and building wealth become something to be avoided rather than achieved. And without wealth, many Christian endeavors would be unattainable.

---

[38] D. Lapin, *Thou Shall Prosper: Ten Commandments for Making Money*, p 17

So what is the purpose of wealth? One very materialistic view is "he who dies with the most toys wins." But, in truth, he who does die with the most toys still dies. The "win" in wealth is not in toys. The win in wealth is found in the purpose of money. In other words, what does God want us to do with our money?

God calls on us to give tithes and offerings (Malachi 3:7-12, Proverbs 3:9-10) to the local church. One of the most worshipful things a believer ever does is give. This is a matter of the heart. This is an act of love. Indeed, we give ourselves first, then we give our wealth – willingly, liberally, cheerfully, regularly, and proportionately (1 Corinthians 9:6-7 and 16:1-2, 2; 2 Corinthians 8:5, 12; 9:7). So the win in wealth is that our giving is greater.

God will often test us with our money. Be ready (Luke 18 and 19, Joshua 7). There are many biblical examples of those who failed the test, and there are those who passed the test. How will you do? Will you excel in the grace of giving? (2 Corinthians 2:8) Have you ever seen a U-Haul behind a hearse? Why do we try to keep that which we cannot keep? The win in a biblical understanding of wealth is passing the test.

God wants us to use our wealth to provide for our families (1 Timothy 5:8). There is great satisfaction and joy in taking care of your immediate family and those in your church family. I doubt if anyone will ever recognize all the social welfare that is provided week after week by local houses of faith. The win in wealth is the ability to care for those you love.

Hospitality is opening your home to those you know and have deep relationships with, and those with whom you have yet to build friendship. It is not about your home's being extravagant or humble; it is about its being used to spread the love of Christ (Romans 12:13). Indeed, wealth allows us to practice the rich tradition of faith, family, and friends in our homes.

And wealth allows us to fund Kingdom business (1 Kings 5-7; Luke 8:1-3). I look back at all the church expansions, Christian universities, missionaries, pregnancy centers, homeless shelters, medical missions, children homes, etc. that I have had the joy to contribute to, and I smile. There is great contentment in being a part of the expansion of God's Kingdom.

Money matters. Wealth in the hands of a righteous man is noble. So whether you are a one-, two-, or five-talent person (Matthew 25:14-30), I pray you will be found faithful. I pray you will show an increase. May you hear the words, "Well done, you took what I gave you and created wealth."

CHAPTER 65: FAILURE TO CLOSE

Show proper respect to everyone ... 1 Peter 2:17a (NIV)

Be careful to respect others. If you do not, it could cost you in more ways than one.

It was New Year's Eve, and I made an offer my wife could not refuse. I told her that I would watch both of our young sons and paint the living room if she would just go and buy a new car for the family. Without hesitation, she took the offer.

When she returned home later, much later than I expected, I was surprised that the new vehicle did not have many of the features we had talked about. Her story reminds all of us how not respecting others can be quite costly.

After visiting several dealerships, she found the car with all the features we had been seeking for the last several months. When the salesman approached, she told him she was ready and wanted the vehicle. He told her, "Honey, you go get your husband, come back, and we will make the deal." My young wife was in shock. She told the salesman, "I have my checkbook. I do not need my husband. Can we go make this deal?" The salesman looked at her with frustration and said for a second time, "Honey, as I told you, go get your husband. Come back. And we can make this deal."

She finished her story by telling me how she then went to a different dealership, one that treated her with respect, promised to add the missing features at the first of year, insisted she take her new vehicle home to her family, told her to enjoy her holiday.

Listening to my wife tell me her experience, I could not help but be proud of her for walking away.

Why do people not respect others? Why do we not treat people appropriately? Can we learn to get past our preconceived notions – and perhaps faulty – idea of what is appropriate? Can we not simply overlook some differences? When we do not respect others, the cost can be lost opportunities.

Treating people with respect is good for all aspects of our lives. Each of us should seek to treat others the way we would prefer to be treated. Whether we are conducting business, dealing with friends or family, or even strangers – each of us should seek to treat others with dignity. To do otherwise is not only harmful to others, but also possibly harmful to ourselves.

And for the record, that New Year's Day was filled with trips in our new car and games in our freshly painted living room.

CHAPTER 66: MAKE YOUR LIST

*I will give thanks to you, Lord, with all my heart; I will tell of all
your wonderful deeds. I will be glad and rejoice in you; I will sing
the praises of your name, O Most High.* Psalm 9:1-2 (NIV)

Social media is flooded with people posting each day for
thirty days what they are thankful for. What a pleasant break
from all the political banter found on the internet of late. While
politics are important, giving thanks is superior.

Most of those reading this column celebrate Thanksgiving
Day with family and friends. Many had more than enough to
eat. Right now many feel especially thankful. Now would be a
good time −and it would be good for your soul, as well − to
write a list of 30 things you are thankful for today.

Consider what you can put on your list as I share a few of
mine.

I am thankful that even though I am the son of a truck
driver, who was the son of a share cropper, I did not realize I
was poor until I was an adult. Family is more than things. Family
is a place to belong. A place to be loved. A place of
unconditional love. Where I learned the value of hard work,
accepting nothing from the government. And where I learned
the delicious taste of chocolate gravy over hot buttered biscuits.

I am thankful for an extended family of seven brothers and
sisters with children, grandchildren, and great grandchildren,
with a wide diversity of political opinions. Positions that many
are very passionate about. And in this diversity are found peace,

acceptance, respect, games, laughter, support, protection, traditions of holiday gatherings, family vacations, and deep love.

It is with deep appreciation and thanksgiving that I observe my adult sons. Their love of life and family is so rewarding. They are so kind in their relationships with others. They work hard and are disciplined. Their faith convictions, while strong, are the perpetual prayer of all parents. And when your son has a wife as amazing as his mother, one is thankful, indeed.

And I am thankful for the pure joy I see in my wife's eyes when she is with our granddaughters. Is there anything more rewarding than seeing those you love so happy with life?

I am thankful for the church, out of which have come many movements that have advanced society. Health care, hospitals, orphanages, food banks, homeless shelters, colleges and universities, business and economic development, arts, child protection, battered women shelters, medical relief such as AIDS intervention, disease prevention, disaster relief, after-school care, adoption, and many more humanitarian efforts and organizations can trace their origins from the church. And the church continues to be a global leader in serving others.

And for this great diverse, pluralistic, society we call America, I give thanks. For there is no other nation where we can freely live. May America always maintain her Christian heritage, for in Christianity all people can live in peace, even those of different faith. Indeed, sadly, that is not possible with all faiths.

I am thankful for work. The jobs I have enjoyed in ministry and the marketplace have provided more than my needs and a few of my wants. To this day, the joy of a job well done brings deep satisfaction. To this day, the pain of failure has taught me more than success ever will.

How about your list? Why not write down all that you are thankful for? A thankful heart is paramount to a good life. As the old hymn says, "Count your blessings, name them one by one."

CHAPTER 67: GRIEF AT CHRISTMAS

Record my misery; list my tears on your scroll – are they not in your record? Psalm 56:8 (NIV)

It is okay to cry at Christmastime as we celebrate life with family and friends. Tears often invade the joy when experiencing certain aromas, songs, or family traditions. Tears often come when certain words are spoken or sung. Emotions can swell, often unexpectedly. Why? It is not because we want to be the Grinch that stole Christmas. It is because we remember. A certain sight, an aroma, or that touch causes us to remember.

For many, life is upside down, even during the holidays. Perhaps their context has changed significantly due to loss. Loss visits us in many forms: divorce, financial loss, death, dreams unfulfilled or denied, tragedy, illness, or separation. Often the loss is recent and fresh. At times the loss occurred years ago. Or, perhaps no matter how hard one has worked, life has not changed for the better. No matter how many times one tries, struggles just do not end. And why should next year be any different? The heart remains broken.

Tears are not a sign of weakness. Tears are not to be avoided. Tears are a gift from God. Tears remind us that, indeed, we are alive. So this Christmas, remember to celebrate with laughter, joy, and even tears, by remembering these truths about that liquid running down your cheeks.

Our tears and our pain are precious to the Lord. Our tears are Christ-like (John 11:35). Tears come when we care deeply. Tears remind us that hurt is beyond reason. What the mind cannot handle, the body will – often in tears. On this side of heaven, tears are a part of life (Ecclesiastes 3:4). There are times when we need to cry. So why do we try to stop our tears? There is a time to embrace the pain, and pain is often healed when it is accepted and embraced.

Remember that our tears are not intended to last forever. Life is hard. Life is not fair. Life is often unbearable. Pain is real in the dark of night. But joy often comes in daybreak (Psalm 30:5). God does not ignore your pain. His ear is attentive to your situation (Psalm 34:15). He knows your hurt. He always knows when you cry. In fact, God records your every tear on a scroll and collects them in a bottle (Psalm 56:8). Your pain is real, and when you cry, God is present.

While tears are a part of this life, your heavenly Fathers longs to wipe away every tear in paradise (Revelations 21:4). There is a place where we will cry no more.

So this holiday, if you find someone around you in tears, instead of telling them to stop crying, walk with them in their tears. Perhaps they are remembering a child whom they have not heard from in many years. Allow them to share or just allow them to cry. Perhaps the person beside you is crying as they sing that Christmas song because someone they loved deeply is singing this year with the angels above. You may or may not know the reason for their tears, but you can be there. Their pain may be too deep to share at that moment. There are no right words for tears. There is a right position. Right where you are. Just be there. Allow the moment.

And if you are the one with watery eyes, please know that God is there with you. He is recording your every tear. He, and He alone, can give you peace in the pain. Know that those around you love you. And if you cannot share why you are crying, just ask them to be with you.

Why do tears make us so uncomfortable? Should we not be more like Christ? Should we not weep at times? Should we not be more like our heavenly father, collecting the tears of those we love?

CHAPTER 68: CHRISTMAS MESSENGER

And there were shepherds living out in the fields nearby, keeping watch over their flocks at night. An angel of the Lord appeared to them . . . Luke 2:8-9b (NIV)

Pause and consider the presence of the angelic host moments after the birth of Jesus. There must have been great excitement such as had never had been felt before in heaven. Possibly the angels had an uncontrollable urge to shout "Hosanna" so that the whole world would know that this child, born only moments ago, was the Son of God.

"But whom shall we tell?" The religious leaders of the day – the Pharisees, Essenes, Sadducees, and Rabbis – were likely considered, but not chosen. Truly wise men from afar were already on their way bringing gifts for the new king of Kings. So, "whom shall we tell?"

As the angels pondered, their orders came. "Go tell of the birth of my son to the shepherds. Let them be the first to tell of the birth of my child."

Why did God choose the shepherds? They, above everyone else in the entire world, were chosen to hear the story of the birth of Christ from the angels. Why the shepherds?

God has a history of using ordinary people, like shepherds ". . . living out in the fields nearby, keeping watch over their flocks at night" (Luke 2:8). The life of a shepherd was simple. Shepherds had no time for theological debates or the cumbersome rules men added to the laws of Moses. The laws of

Moses had become like the laws of our time, so complex that no one could understand them. Shepherds worked long, hard hours in the field. And under the stars at night, they often spent time in prayer and meditation. They were close to God in their hearts, not in their ceremonies. They were just the type of people God often uses when He has something extraordinary to accomplish. We, like the shepherds, should strive for a simple life, a life lived worshipping God in our hearts and not in the motions of our ceremonies.

Like God, shepherds were known to stop everything to care for just one sheep (Matthew 18:13-14). Every sheep mattered enough to the shepherd to leave the warmth and protection of the fire. Our patience is for the lost ones of the world. We must move with compassion into the world. We must patrol the Gates of Hell to keep people from entering.

God saw the shepherds as a group who would be honest messengers. The angels' message to them was, "I bring you good news of great joy that will be for all the people" (Luke 2:10). In their time, shepherds were known as people who were honest and straightforward. Their words did not mean authority, but meant truth. Christians need to display such qualities of honesty and truth in view of others. We must think of the message we carry. We must consider the picture our daily habits are painting.

And God's messenger would need courage. "The shepherds returned, glorifying and praising God for all the things they had heard and seen, which were just as they had been told" (Luke 2:20). The shepherds had courage to seek out the truth during this politically sensitive time. Herod, the king in office, had heard the growing rumor of a new king. Rumors were saying, "For to us a child is born . . . and He will be called Wonderful, Counselor, Mighty God, Everlasting Father, Prince of Peace" (Isaiah 9:6). Such praise and recognition filled Herod with hate. The shepherds knew quite well what might happen if they encountered Herod, but they went anyway.

Indeed, God chose the right messengers. The shepherds listened, investigated, rejoiced, and glorified and praised God while sharing the message. This is the type of person God wants you to be, one who shares the good news of Jesus. Rejoice in the fact that you know the good news of Jesus, but also rejoice in the fact that you can share it.

God trusted the shepherds with the story of the birth of His Son. This Christmas, may you be the type of person God would choose to send angels to in order to share his news. Whom shall you tell?

CHAPTER 69: KEEPING CHRIST IN CHRISTMAS

But the angel said to them, "Do not be afraid. I bring you good news that will cause great joy for all the people. Today in the town of David a Savior has been born to you; he is the Messiah, the Lord. This will be a sign to you: You will find a baby wrapped in cloths and lying in a manger." Luke 2:10-12 (NIV)

So how did you do this holiday season? In all the celebration, lights, parties, programs, gifts, seasonal music, and more - did you and your family maintain the true reason for the most wonderful time of the year? How did you keep Christ in Christmas?

At my family gathering of eight siblings and their children, grandchildren, and more (about 50 people) at least two special things happened that captured the spirit of Christmas.

We have stopped buying gifts for adults for several years because there are just too many people. We only draw names for the children and teens. After the chaos of the children opening gifts and having time to play with their new treasures, a granddaughter crawled up in my lap. Looking at me with great concern and curiosity, she asked, "Poppy, where is your gift?"

And after a rendition of a popular Christmas story, reading of the Biblical account of Jesus' birth, our oldest sibling, Robert, shared this family Christmas prayer he wrote:

Merry Christmas to All and Happy Birthday, Jesus!

Lord, forgive us for our earthly ways.
Often when we first think of Christmas,
We focus on the lights, gifts, food,
And social obligations.

But then a light shines through,
Reminding us of the real reason for Christmas.
We are celebrating a birth,
A special birth, the birth of a Savior.

The real qualities of Christmas are love,
Joy, celebration, devotion, prayer,
And matters of the heart and soul.

One matter of importance is remembering.
We remember the good and the bad,
We can be glad and also sad,
We count our blessings and ache with our sorrows.

But most of all – remember that
God so loved the world that we
Can live in the faith of everlasting joy and love.
So embrace God and each other in the
True meaning of Christmas. Amen.[39]

So reflect on how you remembered Christ this holiday season with family and friends. Decide today to keep Christ in each and every day in the year ahead. For the story of Christ is great news. And His story can bring great joy for all people. Let's spread the joy to everyone.

---

[39] Poem by Robert L. Perkins, Jr., Christmas 2016.

ABOUT THE AUTHOR

D. Clay Perkins, Ph. D., is an energetic, positive, and encouraging servant in God's Kingdom. Dr. Perkins has been in the ministry since 1979 serving both small and large churches. In 2006 he became President of Mid-Atlantic Christian University, Legacy Roanoke Bible College and Eastern Christian College, in Elizabeth City, NC. Ordained at Pinedale Christian Church in Winston-Salem, NC, Perkins has served at Peachcrest Christian Church in Decatur, GA; Hickory Lane Church of Christ in Washington Court House, OH; Piedmont Christian Church in Greensboro, NC; and First Christian Church Ministries in Kernersville, NC.

Dr. Perkins has degrees from Point University, Cincinnati Christian University, and Regent University - School of Business and Leadership. His business background includes owning and operating The Time Gallery, Inc. and Perkins Services Group, Inc.

As President of Mid-Atlantic Christian University, Dr. Perkins' duties encompass strategic planning, management, fund raising, promotion, and oversight to the university. He has a major role in training extraordinary leaders for Kingdom work. Clay enjoys teaching leadership courses at Mid-Atlantic and other universities amid his other obligations.

Perkins serves on boards for HASTEN International and Financial Planning Ministries. He is involved in the local community as a Rotarian. Clay and his wife Sandra worship at Journey Christian Church in Elizabeth City. They have two sons, Daniel and Benjamin. Clay's favorite title is "Poppy" to granddaughters Evelyn and Ruby.

Visit Clay's social media posts at Facebook.com/drdclayperkins and Twitter.com/dclayperkins

Made in the USA
Las Vegas, NV
26 February 2022

44628009R00095